VICTORIAN PORTRAITS:

HOPKINS AND PATER

Victorian Portraits:
Hopkins and Pater

by

David Anthony Downes

BOOKMAN ASSOCIATES, Inc.

NEW YORK 3

In memory of our late beloved President:

JOHN FITZGERALD KENNEDY

Preface

GERARD MANLEY HOPKINS and Walter Horatio Pater were friends,
yet no one has really cared to consider the significance of their
friendship. In the ensuing essays, I hope to have made a beginning, and in so doing, I have been deeply aware that Pater and
Hopkins are not only important witnesses to their own times,
but in the breadth of their spirits they have given us some of
the first glimpses of our own world. Therefore, what they saw
and thought and dreamed of takes on added meaning in trying
to understand them and ourselves. My essays, then, are intended
to form a composite of two Victorians in and out of their times
who, despite the fact that they lived and died well within the
last century, saw the road leading to our century and some of
the crossroads we would have to confront. In a few instances
they left us some milestones by which to choose or change our
way.

There are some fresh views about Hopkins and Pater which
have needed emphasis in order to refocus critical attitudes towards them. For instance, we have heard a great deal about
Hopkins, the ascetic priest, the Catholic apologete, and the
neurotic poet. But it was not only Catholicism, the Jesuits, and
Scotus which influenced him as a writer; there was also the
literary swell of the Romantic Movement which marked profoundly and lastingly his literary personality. I have tried to
examine Hopkins' Romanticism both in its Christian and Victorian trappings. To be sure Hopkins' Romanticism was his own
brand, as indeed were Wordsworth's and Keats'; nevertheless,
I have tried to show that however traditional his mind, his was
a Romantic heart.

Also a long-held attitude about Pater is confronted in these essays—Pater, the anti-Christian ritualist. I have attempted to indicate a process of religious development in Pater which brought him to a new religious assent based upon his personal experience. The outline of this development, I argue, is evident in *Marius The Epicurean* which I read as a kind of phenomenology of religious belief with certain cogent parallels with Newman's *Grammar of Assent*. Hard-core Paterians will ask whether I am asserting that Pater became an orthodox Christian, and if so, why his writings after *Marius* are not explicitly Christian. I answer that Pater worked his way to a deeply personal image of God and a real assent to the proposition that He exists. There is no reason to doubt that the religious context of his belief was not Christian, for there is no evidence at all that for Pater religion meant anything else than Christianity. However, Pater's Christian assent is best described as that kind of belief found in the early Church of the Apostles and Martyrs, that is, a deeply personal, communal, liturgical, pastoral faith with only the slightest theological development. Pater's great difficulty was with the evolution of the notional level of Christianity—theology. Here his own temper of mind split his inferences from his religious assent. Still he grappled because he knew that the wholeness of faith had a notional as well as a real and personal basis. Moreover, his religious predicament was not an unusual one for a Christian then or now. There are numerous instances in which a Christian has rational doubt about his understanding of what he believes. Pater had to encounter the difficult and disconcerting lesson all Christians have to learn, in Newman's words: ". . . to be just able to doubt is no warrant for disbelieving." As for Pater's later writings, I see no heavy negation of my attitude resulting from the absence of Christian apologetics in them. In many, religious interests would be out of place; in others, Pater addresses himself to whatever religious questions seem apt. His review of *Robert Elsmere* and his essay on Pascal are examples. His personality and his religious temper did not allow for kerygmatic pronouncements.

There is a question touching both Hopkins and Pater which some might think I have avoided. This is the issue of their being homosexual. Students of both men discuss this possibility and the implications it might have had on their life and works. The evidence I have seen is so conjectural that I see no reason to treat the question seriously. While I do not rule out the possibility of certain latent homosexual tendencies in each, I have found nothing of consequence resulting from this speculation. It is a dead end and thus I have not bothered with it.

I wish to express my sincere gratitude to the following who have helped me in the writing of this book: Lawrence G. Evans who put his enormous Paterian knowledge and material at my disposal generously and graciously; Father D. A. Bischoff, S.J., whose scholarly friendship for me is exceeded only by his for Hopkins; Father John A. Fitterer, S.J., Dean of Arts and Sciences at Seattle University who has generously granted me leave and lessened my duties to further my work; to the Research Committee at Seattle University for its helpful grant to carry out this study; to my colleagues for their critical readings, especially Father Robert Carmody, S. J.; and to all the libraries and publishers herein cited for the "fair use" of their materials. While I am indebted to all of the above, of course, what has been said and done within these covers is entirely my responsibility.

D. A. DOWNES

Seattle,
November, 1964

Contents

Contents

CHAPTER I

Victorian Sketches

IT HAS BEEN FREQUENTLY SAID that Gerard Hopkins and Walter Pater were friends. The statement is a true one, though exactly what it means, perhaps, will never be known. This is not only so because it seems that materials for Pater's biography are forever lost; there is also Hopkins' troubled dream of art abandoned. These with time cast very long shadows. Still shadows are not without contours, and it is intriguing how very often their general shapes harmonize.

Both Pater and Hopkins were men who were constitutionally onlookers; reflection and imagination were the main qualities of their persons. There is a sense of life that is primarily a state of consciousness, just as there is life which is largely the contact of action—practical judgment being its highest point of awareness. Pater and Hopkins lived intense inner lives. Their powers were mainly directed towards the total apprehension of experience. Thus they had the characteristic attribute of such personalities, which is imaginative enactment with its rich overtones of deep feeling. Art and religion quite naturally claimed their most earnest attentions, particularly those sorts which are highly ritualistic in mode and individualistic in style. These conveyed life vividly to them and deployed their own experiences meaningfully.

But to the physically inert, the life of action is often most admirable. This admiration is from afar and is cast into some form of artifice where it can calmly be appreciated. In Hopkins and Pater, this took the form of delight in the Classic and Chivalric figures in Western art, idealized figures of high imagination rendered with markedly distinctive touches of their creators—the monumentality of Michelangelo and the daring poetic heightening of Milton's *Samson Agonistes*. This respect for physical power, of course, is always modulated by their personal tempers: Pater usually finds a soft sweetness nesting in strength and Hopkins a spiritual tenderness.

There is in Hopkins and Pater a sort of riotous living of the beauty of things. It seems from the outside a wholesale revelry of the kind captured in Keats' "Ode to a Nightingale." Yet outwardly both Hopkins and Pater lived very sober lives, a quiet falling of dust. Their true personalities remained recessive and obscure; their demeanor suggested taut restraint beneath voracious interests. But their high moments manifest themselves with blinding brightness of which they talk as if they were ascetic monks. Such contrasts are open to strong and suspicious curiosities; they are liable to parody as well. So there is some point to Mallock's satirical portrait of Pater in *The New Republic* just as the Jesuit Provincial's dilemma of what to do with Father Hopkins had a truthful side even when reduced to the level of recreation-room humor.

These men possessed poetic personalities, which is to say that they had a different relation with words from people in general and writers particularly. This is a question of sensitivity, which is as much innate as learned, whose implications bear heavily upon the degree to which words become identified with the deployments of various states of consciousness. The heightening and fixing powers of verbal orders Coleridge described as a "fusing" action in which there takes place a transmutation of experience and emotion into very complex expressive forms. Objective and subjective become interfused into a medium wherein the poet is refined into identity. This is the sort of individuation which Hopkins and Pater sought in their writings; it is the kind of distinction they most appreciated in the works of others. In general, then, words were a special way of life for them in a manner quite different from that relation between language and personality which normally obtains. This explains Pater's pious disciplinary process of composition and Hopkins' great and delicate tenderness for his compositions. Here their very souls were magnified.

Of course, personalities so expressible often take voice early, and while the mode is frequently mere verbal effervescence, the effusion reveals the kinds of sensible life which have stored up to spill over into the plenty of a poem. Hopkins is by now famous for his artistic granaries, and we have his first productions as signs and shapes of the future. Regarding Pater, we have Thomas Wright's and William Sharp's assurance that Pater wrote a good deal as a young man, including numerous translations and essays, "scores of poems."[1] Wright provides a few brief quotations as well as summaries of these poems, and while most has been lost, it is possible to obtain some impression of Pater's early development.

Both Hopkins and Pater as fledgling poets strongly felt the denseness of the beauty of things. This sensitivity is probably peculiar to the beginner. The difference lies in the quality of felt perception. In Hopkins and Pater, the distinguishing note is the death of beauty, that is to say, the death of consciousness. So the elusiveness of beauty for them is a tension between the self and the beautiful. There is thus a kind of ratio of pain and perception. In recounting from a distance his early development, Pater noted the growth of "An almost diseased sensibility to the spectacle of suffering . . ." along with ". . . a more than customary sensuousness. . . ." Hopkins in an early lyric, "Spring and Death," which anticipates the choice charm of his "Spring and Fall," speaks of "—A little sickness in the air/ From too much fragrance everywhere. . . ."

Thus the mortality of beauty led both writers to constant presentiments of death. Pater wrote: "For with this desire of physical beauty mingled itself early the fear of death—the fear of death intensified by the desire of beauty." This is exactly the tenor of Hopkins' "A Vision of Mermaids" in which he richly depicts the bower of beauty the earth is to his eye. This brings in a "sweet sadness" which mothers an insight: ". . . that it is a pain/ To know the dusk depths of the ponderous sea. . . ."[2] This sensibility brought about what Pater called a "biblical awe" into his perspectives which soon became a mediator over his sense of a beautiful world slipping away. The same is quite true for Hopkins. Both saw natural existence from the side of lost beauty.

There is thus in their early development a strong spiritualizing element. This more often than not was the occasion of writing verse explicitly religious. According to Wright, Pater's earliest poem (January, 1856) was "St. Elizabeth of Hungary" in which Pater rather freely recounts her story, ending on a strongly religious note: "With her lamp there brightly burned a pure ethereal flame,/ And so she waited till the great Celestial Bridegroom came." The next poem Wright mentions is "The Chant of the Celestial Sailors" which he describes as the song of Christian pilgrims journeying to heaven. In this as in the previous poem, there is apparently a kind of destined transcendence where the rough is strangely made smooth and the crooked straight.

A perusal of Hopkins' early verse leaves the impression that from the beginning he wrote nothing but religious poems. His "The Habit of Perfection" may be taken as strikingly similar to St. Elizabeth's state of soul as she prepared for the marriage feast when ". . . lily-coloured clothes provide/ Your spouse not laboured-at nor spun." "Heaven-Haven" is a kind of spiritual aspiration of Christian pilgrims wherein a very similar transcendence of this life is sought as that which seems to have been the quality of Pater's "Chant": ". . . out of the swing of the sea." There is a deep intent in Hopkins' early poems to find what saves mortal beauty. This amounts to the question of personal salvation. As Pater wrote in 1858: "Watchman, what of the night? So asks my soul/ In whisper'd fear. Watchman, what of the night?"[3]

The answer to this question has both aesthetic and religious implications. This is another way of saying that there is a correlation between the beautiful and the good. Perhaps the best expression Pater gave to this higher integration was in his

"Diaphaneitè." In this early essay he attempted to give some sense of that especial nature which comes to "repose and simplicity" before the world's groan and grind: "Like all higher forms of inward life this character is a subtle blending and interpenetration of intellectual, moral and spiritual elements."[4] The saving of beauty is a process of purity. The senses must be chastened to the point of crystalline perfection. But this requires a special character. Some purifying power must be at work on the senses. As Pater put it, "It is a mind of taste lighted up by some spiritual ray within."[5] The sight and insight afforded by such a spirit is a remarkable apprehension of reality:

It seeks to value everything at its eternal worth, not adding to it, or taking from it, the amount of influence it may have for or against its own special scheme of life. It is the spirit that sees external circumstances as they are, its own power and tendencies as they are, and realizes the given conditions of its life, not disquieted by the desire for change, or the preference of one part in life rather than another, or passion, or opinion.[6]

Hopkins called this "being in earnest with . . . reality."[7] He showed it in action in his dialogue "On the Origin of Beauty." It is a touchstone of all great art.

The proper serving of beauty depends on a religious system. Pater wrote: "But the character we have before us is a kind of prophecy of this repose and simplicity, coming as it were in the order of grace, not of nature, by some happy gift . . . showing that it is indeed within the limits of man's destiny."[8] To both Hopkins and Pater this "spiritual ray within" was Christianity. Pater began his delineation of the diaphanous character by quoting Thomas à Kempis: " 'Sibi unitus et simplificatus esse,' that is the long struggle of the Imitatio Christi."[9] Hopkins and Pater really put to the test John Ruskin's touchstone, "To see clearly is poetry, prophecy and religion all in one." This is the true story of their lives and their art.

However systemic a theology is, religion depends upon faith. In their day, the faithful were in the doldrums. Added to personal problems of disbelief and sin was a withdrawal of culture's sustaining powers. Pater noted: "The saint, the artist, even the speculative thinker, out of the world's order as they are, yet work, so far as they work at all, in and by means of the main current of the world's energy."[10] Pater's call in his youthful poem, "Down, down I sink. Oh! let me live in Thee,/ Or deep in hell—it seems so awful not to be,"[11] represents more than a terrible sense of personal inadequacy; it is also a distress call from the wreck of religious doubt, as Hopkins wrote: "Our prayer seems lost in desert ways. . . ."[12]

Victorian religious dilemmas cast the darkest shadows over Pater and Hopkins. Both were in the main stream of Christianity. Pater had Catholicism in his background, and while his own upbringing was Anglican, all his life he remained but partially "reformed," insofar as he remained Christian at all. Hopkins' conversion to Catholicism was the main event of his life. There is a very distinct religious quality to their early lives which leads to their more or less defined positions. Pater had an early fascination for the clerical life with its emphasis on celibacy and purity which stayed with him through his college days. A sincere belief in Christ seems to have been taking hold within his large interest in church ritual. He recognized a meaning in ceremony in which he was personally involved. Wright noted: "When home for his holidays, Pater, who (in the words of a cousin) was a 'tremendous Ritualist,' would never eat meat in Lent, and his deportment towards those who did was cold and constrained. The Breviary was as much his companion as the Prayer Book, and every night he said the prayer for peace. . . ." One is reminded of the passage in Hopkins' *Journals* where he prescribes his Lenten discipline.[13]

There is a kind of style to Pater and Hopkins' idea of the Christian life. They wanted to live it on a very high plane of purity, and the self-discipline which this demanded was to be embraced with a nobility of mind as well as graciousness of manner. The true Christian state was a moral probity manifested primarily by grandness of action. Thus the attainment of Christian spiritual ideals was as much a question of beauty as it was of belief.

The beauty that is revealed by art or nature is the result of the actions of great souls or Divinity itself. Thus beauty is the revealed form of a spiritual status or attainment. That is what produced the splendor, and full appreciation demands correlative aspirations. So it may be said that both Pater and Hopkins understood aesthetic implications within the religious state. It is precisely this rare interpenetration of grace and sensibility which was to each a living example of true Christian life. This is what Keble meant to Pater and Newman to Hopkins. Their lights shone through the controversial mental debris of their day. Inspiration also came from those rare geniuses, now long gone, whose lives and art represent high achievements still proclaiming their monumental excellences and perfections. This is really what Pater's *Renaissance* is all about, and it became central to Hopkins' ideal of the Christian priesthood. There are those great human beacons casting their lights from the dead past which can enkindle a new life out of an old radiance. Seldom it is that either Hopkins or Pater ever talk about their art and beauty without coming to the spiritual implications of the sensibility in question. In one sense, art always encompasses religious experience and religion is made remarkable by aesthetics.

What, then, were the great artists reaching out to? Hopkins and Pater could not get away from some notion of archetypal beauty, some high and perfect quiddity to which their creative powers were striving to give sensible form. They, like the great traditionalists before them, looked to Plato for the transcendent qualities of art and life while heeding the "making" processes described by Aristotle. The question was the degree to which the Platonic ideal could be integrated into Christian supernatural life. This is another way of asking how much of an intuitive presentiment of Christianity was in Platonism? Their personal answer to the question is a sharp divider. On the surface it seems that Hopkins had to resign art to be saved and Pater had to resign religion: both, however, demanded absolute fulfillments of their chosen ways which involved that which they sacrificed. Thus, while Pater seems the priest of art and Hopkins of religion, in many ways their total perspectives confound their chosen categories.

The history of their minds is largely a story of this antimony. Cast into a trope, Hopkins spent most of his life in the chapel on the second floor of the house. His eyes and ears were filled with the sounds of life downstairs which, often against his choices, drew him near the stairwell. Having come up, he could not go down again, yet his spirit demanded a full realization of the dual sources of life—upper and lower. His life was largely an arduous effort to live by his decision to go upstairs; his intellectual life was an attempt to justify the spiritual heights of the upper with the sensuous depths of the lower; his artistic life was an intense experiencing through the imagination of split-level living. Hopkins was forever going downstairs to live.

Pater's living room on the first floor was a museum containing the masterworks of great souls. The intervals of beauty they caught filled him with a sense of a higher life which, frequently against his reason, brought him to the foot of the stairs. Having been there before, he could not go up, though his temper required that the exquisite moments on the lower level be somehow permanently reprieved on the upper. His life was mostly an assiduous exertion to live exquisitely his indecision downstairs; his intellectual life was a rich isolation of the spiritual heights of the upper which he found passing within the deep sensuousness of lower existence. His artistic life was a passionate response to the productions of dual-visioned imaginations. Pater was forever coming upstairs to pray.

Even considering the exaggeration of the figure, the internal contradictions suggested find some basis of truth in the lives of Hopkins and Pater. Both lived life at odds. There is the impression that their lives were entangled with more than the usual hesitations, inertias, and ineffectivenesses. They seem always on the brink of life. Set side by side, their personal and professional lives seem to be unspectacular failures. Their quiet desuetude was but the surface of a fierce but silent inner ravage. For this reason art was for them more than an exercise of a disciplined faculty; rather it was a stay against great and hostile life forces. The alternative was collapse.

Such a vital medium of life assumes a special relation to personality. It may become an *alter ego*. Then both person and poem take on double identities. The tensions of art mix with those of life so that there takes place a kind of interpenetration through which life is transmuted into artifice and artifice into life. There results a kind of psychic and spiritual levitation in which the resources of living depend upon real and artificial springs. The soul in suspension looms in the middle. The shades of Pater and Hopkins do seem more than usually bilocated. Perhaps this accounts for a dark weariness in their lives; it may as well be the price for the discovery of another land of lights. Wherever the truth lies, it remains hidden in the shadowy interiors of their deep spirits. Thankfully they have left us some brilliant flashes from out of those depths.

CHAPTER II

Profile of a Friendship

I

GERARD MANLEY HOPKINS went up to Balliol in the Trinity Term, 1863; Walter Horatio Pater became a Fellow of Bresenose in 1864. The earliest record of their acquaintance is 1866 when Hopkins records in his *Journal* for May 2, "Coaching with W. H. Pater this term. Walked with him on Monday evening last, April 30. Fine evening, bitterly cold."[1] The somewhat formal reference to Pater suggests that this was Hopkins' first real contact with the man. After this, he refers simply to Pater. The editors of his papers conjecture that it is possible that Hopkins' essay, "The Origin of our Moral Ideas," was written for Pater in 1865, but the notebook in which it is found is undated. The basis of this speculation is another essay in a different notebook entitled, "On the Origin of Beauty: A Platonic Dialogue," which is dated May 12, 1865. While there is a slim parallel and the implications of the two essays may very well have been topics of conversation between Pater and Hopkins, there is no definitive evidence.

How Hopkins was led to Pater we do not know. Perhaps it was Benjamin Jowett, his tutor, who thought highly of Pater as an undergraduate. It may have been that Hopkins had heard that Pater had offered his time and attentions to the essays of any students interested in availing themselves of the opportunity. We have some idea what coaching was like with Pater. When the student arrived at his incommodious rooms at Brasenose, Pater would interrupt whatever he was doing, place the student in his favorite chair, take a position near his windows, and then ask the student to commence with his essay. His reaction to some quality of the essay was sometimes visible. T. Humphry Ward recalled Pater at these moments:

His ideas, his view of life, were fresh and original, as all the world recognized a few years later; and his criticism of style, though administered with the lightest possible touch, was convincing and final. Vulgarity of expression, over-emphasis, exaggeration, could not stand up for a moment before his correcting pencil; they shrivelled up at a word, and a word was all he gave them. Perhaps he seemed to undervalue learning as such, but no man demanded more clear and accurate thinking, or a more exact expression of it in words. Such is the most definite impression left upon the mind of one who was his pupil in those early years before the world knew him, and before his twenty years of literary eminence had begun.[2]

As Hopkins' journal entry notes, all meetings with Pater did not take place in his rooms. An inveterate walker as his friends and traveling companions remember, Pater often shared his jaunts with students. It is not too much to suppose that at these times he discussed his views on beauty and morality, his antipathies towards scholastic metaphysics, the challenge of scientific skepticism, and the intellectual sterility of the Christian tradition in his times. These are likely topics, for what was on Pater's mind is revealed in his essay, "Coleridge's Writings," which had appeared in the *Westminster Review* five months earlier. In this essay, Pater considers Coleridge as a philosopher (he was later to add a fragment on Coleridge's poetry taken from a biographical introduction he contributed to Ward's *English Poets* in 1883, when this essay was reprinted in *Appreciations* in 1889), but the main interest of the essay is that Pater's own philosophical views are here revealed for the first time.

The essay opens with a judgment as to the nature of modern thought which is then placed in historical context. This, then, becomes the basis for trying Coleridge's philosophic views: "Modern thought is distinguished from ancient by its cultivation of the 'relative' spirit in place of the 'absolute.' Ancient philosophy sought to arrest every object in an eternal outline, to fix thought in a necessary formula, and types of life in a classification of 'kinds' or genera. To the modern spirit nothing is or can be rightly known except relatively under conditions."[3] This "modern spirit" permeates the whole essay so that it becomes clear that metaphysical absolutes are for Pater of slight interest and value.

Furthermore, the modern temper has had its impact on the moral world: "The moral world is ever in contact with the physical; the relative spirit has invaded moral philosophy from the ground of the inductive sciences. There has started anew analysis of the relations of body and mind, good and evil, freedom and necessity."[4] What is interesting here is not that Pater seems to agree with David Hume. That which must have interested his walking companions was where Pater laid the basis of conduct and whether that basis had any Christian implications.

It is wonderful to surmise the conversation between Hopkins and Pater on that bleak, cold Monday evening in April. Hopkins was in the throes of his conversion to Catholicism; some six months later he was to rush to Newman to be received. Hopkins' dilemma was exactly what Pater had mentioned in his Coleridge essay as the trial of their day, for Pater saw the Roman Catholic Church as dividing man's spirit between the human and divine: one side is faith transcending this life; the other side, ". . . all that is desirable in this world. . . ." Significantly, Pater then saw many intermediate positions though ". . . time eventually is a dogmatist, working out the opposition in the most trenchant form, and fixing the horns of the dilemma." Whatever was said did not quell Hopkins' Romanist bent, and Pater may very well have made some remarks very provocative to an intense young spirit bent on buckling himself to supernaturalism. Pater wrote in the 1866 essay, "A transcendentalism that makes what is abstract more excellent than what is concrete has nothing akin to the leading philosophies of the world."[5] It is in some ways a little astonishing that the man who wrote this was admired as a Platonist! Pater later suggests that this tension between categories and the senses has subsisted "ever since the dawn of the Renaissance" as a conflict between reason and faith: "From the first, indeed, the Christian religion has affirmed the existence of such a conflict, and had even based its plea upon its own weakness in it. In the face of the Classical culture, with its deep wide-struck roots in the world as it permanently exists, St. Paul asserted the claims of that which could not appeal with success to any genuinely human principle." Such talk may have made that evening bleaker and colder for Hopkins.

That they could have had a fruitful discussion of theology is doubtful. By this time Pater had ceased to accept Christian theology though his enigmatic religious attitudes leave much doubt about his state of disbelief. It is clear that he had not lost interest in religion, but, as his essay forthrightly shows, theology offered him but an occasion of dismissal:

Theology is a great house, scored all over with hieroglyphics by perished hands. When we decypher one of these hieroglyphics, we find in it the statement of mistaken opinion; but knowledge has crept onward since the hand dropped from the wall; we no longer entertain the opinions, and we can trace the origin of the mistake. Dogmas are precious as memorials of a class of sincere and beautiful spirits, who in a past age of humanity struggled with many tears, if not for true knowledge, yet for a noble and elevated happiness.[6]

How does one treat the occurrence of theology in the minds of men? Pater urged an historical approach which, if the two touched on the subject, might have caused Pater to repeat his historical perspective on that theological tradition which Hopkins was about to accept: "The weakness of these dogmas had ever been not so much a failure of the authority of Scripture or tradition in their favour, as their conflict with the reason that they were words rather than conceptions. That analysis of words and conceptions which in modern philosophy has been a principle of continual rejuvenescence with Descartes and Berkeley, as well as with Bacon and Locke, had desolated the field of scholastic theology."[7] If these remarks did pass, they could not but have provoked Hopkins into revealing his rather aromatic religious spirit which burnt like incense in the sanctuary of Christianity. Pater's reaction may have been a quiet pity or envy. Perhaps he felt like Marius when, on his way to Cecilia's household, he hears singing in the church: "It was the expression not altogether of mirth, yet of some wonderful sort of happiness. . . ."[8]

It is not improbable to surmise that these two young men never got beyond art. While there is no convincing evidence that Hopkins actually wrote his Platonic dialogue on beauty for Pater, there is no better evidence that he did not. Hopkins had written in the essay on moral ideas "for W. H. Pater, Esq.," that "Beauty lies in the relation of the parts of a sensuous thing to each other. . . ." The occasion of this statement was Hopkins' attempt to draw an analogy between beauty and moral excellence. While Pater had in general little interest in artistic theories, the relations between the aesthetic experience and a moral system were engaging to him. His critical appreciations never definitively draw up his position, but from the first essay on, they most assertively maintain the integrity of the aesthetic elements in the artistic experience: "Doubtless, the idea, the intellectual element, is the spirit and life of art. Still, art is the triumph of the senses and the emotions; and the senses and the emotions must not be cheated of their triumph after all."

The same thesis about beauty as a relationship of sensuous parts is taken up by Hopkins in his Platonic dialogue, this time solely to consider the origin and nature of beauty. Pater and Hopkins could have gone on at length on Hopkins' ideas of "chromatic and diatonic beauty."[9] Indeed the essay is rife with topics which very well may have entirely occupied the two in many a conversation: the difference between prose and poetry (verse employs "a continuous structural parallelism"); the act of artistic creation (an act of travail and agony for Pater but in which Hopkins found that, ". . . the idea rose in the forms of expression. . . ."); the relation between the poet's personality and the poem (". . . that the concentration, the intensity, which is called in by means of an artificial structure brings into play the resources of genius. . . .").[10]

It is not too much to suggest that there is a passage in the dialogue which has a definite Paterian temper to it and if Pater saw it, he would very likely have been pleasingly amused:

I foresee I shall be told a string of sublime unlaborious definitions of poetry, that Poetry is this and Poetry is that, and that I am not to vex the Poet's mind with my shallow wit, for I cannot fathom it, and that the divine faculty is not to be degraded to the microscope and the dissecting knife, and wherever a flower expands and dedicates its beauty to the sun there, there is Poetry, and that I am a Positivist (as I do not object to be called in a way), and that I am a fingering slave and would peep and botanize upon my mother's grave, and that I am the carrion vulture and wait, or do not wait, to tear the Poet's heart before the crowd, and that I am a Philistine of an aggravated specious kind, and that Shakespere [sic] and Wordsworth and Tennyson and many others have uttered curses on me, and that my reward will be that I shall be cankered and rivelled together and crisped up by the hate of hate, the scorn of scorn, which the Poet, the emphatic authentic ideal Poet, will treat me with. Dear me, I seem to myself to have become poetically and vividly descriptive of that last effect in my energetic forecast. Yes, I see it all with a glassy countenance. And you who made such flattering promises have cast the first stone. But do your worst: let me spell *poet* with a little *p* and perish.[11]

Robert Bridges in his memoir of Hopkins notes that the latter, in preparing for his Classical first class, ". . . enjoyed the sympathetic tuition of Walter Pater." While *tuition* may be technically inaccurate, *sympathetic* can be accepted as an element in their relationship for which there was a basis from the start.[12]

II

In that same journal entry of May 2, 1866, Hopkins jotted, "Same evening Hexameron met here: Addis read on the Franciscans: laughter. Thought all the next day of the terrible history of Fra Dolcino."[13] The Hexameron was an essay society (so called because it met six days a term) to which Hopkins belonged and for which it is probable that he read at least one paper. He wrote to his friend, A. W. M. Baillie on September 10, 1864, "I am meditating an essay, perhaps for the *Hexameron*, on some points of poetical criticism. . . ."[14] He goes on in his letter to discuss the language of verse which could have been the gist of his essay. Four months later on January 5, 1865: "I am now toiling through an essay for the Hexameron, but can you tell me what in music answers to realism in painting. The other arts seem to depend on truth (no: Truth) as well as Beauty. What then answers to, I mean what is, Truth in music? Blow me an answer from thy wreathed horn."[15]

An Oxford Vade Mecum throngs with clubs, societies, dinners, and teas (high or low) because traditional English university education is personal, informal, social, and unadministered. This was very likely more true in Hopkins' day. Their virtue is that they provide that social finesse which is the dress of the fully cultivated mind. The art of civilized conversation demands, however, a high plane of ideas as well as the play of the mind, a necessity some organizations seem never to obtain and others deliberately avoid.

These activities highlight a young man's emerging personality, often with an amazing prototypic accuracy, as is the case with Hopkins. So far as is known, he considered one other society for which he was put up, but which he never finally joined.[16] This was the Brotherhood of the Holy Trinity, a High Church Society of Oxford dons and undergraduates. Started as a group interested in ecclesiastical art in 1844, it was turned into a kind of lay apostolate and functioned for over forty years. When Hopkins went up to Oxford, the society was under the inspiration of Dr. Pusey who had provided quasi-monastic rules of a voluntary nature. Many of Hopkins' later friends had joined already. In December of 1863, Hopkins, W. Addis, and Robert Bridges among others were proposed and elected on January 28, 1864. Hopkins, tempted though he was, never joined, probably under his parents' advice.[17] Moreover, as his diary indicates, he was privately living a much more ascetic life than the Brotherhood encouraged.[18]

Hopkins was a member of the Hexameron Society. This organization was founded by H. P. Liddon in March of 1864: "I hope that we have got together a sufficient body of clever men to make our Club intellectually respectable, and it will open next Term with an introductory essay on the relations of Theology to Philosophy. . . ." Eight organization and procedural rules were drawn up at the first meeting, the name Hexameron was adopted, the Reverend Liddon was named president. The first rule was the critical one or the "test" as S. R. Brooke, the secretary, wrote to Liddon regarding the first meeting: "The object of the —— Essay Society shall be to promote discussions upon subjects of interest so far as may be consistent with adherence to the doctrines of the Catholic Faith."[19] Hopkins apparently was involved in the society from its earliest stages of formation. He listed in his *Journal* for March 1864 a series of "new names" which, it is highly probable, refers to the Hexameron membership.

There is extant in the Bodleian Library[20] a printed list of members and rules. The membership list is dated Act Term, 1865. It contains most of Hopkins' closest friends and associates. Notably absent is Robert Bridges. Also extant at the Bodleian are three printed notices of meetings which S. R. Brooke used to notify members of coming meetings. In addition to designating the members' rooms, the day, and the date, there is a place for the topic of the essay to be read. Only two of these are filled in. One subject announced is "Bigotry (W. Challis)" and the other, "Democracy, its nature and effects." None of the essays among Hopkins' papers can be certainly designated as having been read to the Hexameron Society. There is speculation that his Platonic dialogue, "On the Origin of Beauty" may have been written for this purpose, though its length precludes any strong probability.

The purpose of this society was to propagate belief. There were clubs which seemed to stand for unbelief. In a letter which W. Addis wrote to enlist a student of Queen's, J. R. Madan, as a member of the Hexameron Society, he mentioned an opponent while stating one of the objectives of the society: "To preserve men who come up with good church feeling and a disposition to lead from the snare of such societies as the 'old mortality' which almost avowedly formed themselves on the denial of much which is dear to all of us." There is a printed sheet in the Bodleian titled, "The Old Mortality." This is a "rough list" of members from 1856 through 1866 headed by a brief note on the founding and nature of the club:

This Society was founded (as appears from the Minute Books) in November, 1856, in the rooms of John Nichol, of Balliol College, and on his suggestion, for the purpose of affording its members "such intellectual pastime and recreation as should seem most suitable and agreeable." Its name was derived "from the following weighty consideration: That every member of the aforesaid Society was, or lately had been, in so weak and precarious a condition of bodily health as plainly and manifestly to instance the great frailty, and, so to speak, mortality, of this our human life and constitution." A body of twenty rules was adopted at a meeting held on the 2nd of May, 1857, when discussion turned on Hume's Essay in defence of Suicide.

Among the notable names listed are A. C. Swinburne, Balliol (1856); Pater's one-time pupil-friend-traveling companion-literary executor, C. L. Shadwell, Christ Church (1861); W. H. Pater, Queen's (1862-1866?); and the Honorable Secretary of the Hexameron Society, S. R. Brooke, Corpus Christi (1862-1866?).

The question is whether this throws any light on Hopkins' and Pater's relationship through the Hexameron Society. Twenty-nine days after the entry about being coached by Pater, Hopkins wrote, among other things, after the date of May 31: "A little rain and at evening and night hard rain.—Pater talking two hours against Xtianity."[21] Could this entry possibly refer to a paper which Pater read at an Hexameron meeting? It seems doubtful. There is some evidence that Pater was becoming known about this time for his heterodox views on such matters as the immortality of the soul and the possibility of a future life, but where Hopkins heard him expatiate is not clear.[22] What is evident is that Hopkins did hear Pater out on Christianity, and what is significant is that Pater's disavowal did not seem to influence either Hopkins' conversion or his friendship for Pater. Both become parts of Hopkins' life.

III

The role of his conversion is now common knowledge of Hopkins' life; the friendship with Pater is not. The documentation of their relationship is unfortunately one-sided because, as Edmund Gosse noted, Pater kept no diary, wrote few letters, preserved no records of his friends and experiences.[23] Hopkins was quite the opposite as the world knows, and while references to Pater do not stand out in his letters and papers, they are there, sprinkled at such salient points that it is not too much to observe that their friendship lasted all of Hopkins' life. The record is perhaps more implicit than explicit, though what record there is shows an intimacy and care for each other which is rather astonishing for a shy, reticent scholar-artist and a self-silenced, ascetic priest-poet.

As Hopkins would say, the instress of Pater on his own life is revealed from the very first. Pater's way of looking at things and expressing his impressions had become a mannerism for Hopkins. In a letter not long after the May entries in his *Journal*, Hopkins wrote on June 30, 1866 to his friend, W. A. Comyn Macfarlane, regarding choice English spots: "The Sussex downs are seductive as Pater says, if there is a church."[24] The words *seductive* and *church* are typical associations of Pater's sensibilities, apparently a conjunction that had stuck in young Hopkins' mind. While to the staidly orthodox, the association of sensuous and religious experiences may come as a shock, as indeed they did to Father Hopkins' superiors when they heard or read some of his sermons;[25] Hopkins knew what Pater meant and shared his awareness. They are some of the most self-revelatory moments in his sermons.

In the spring of 1867, Hopkins took his degree. That Easter he spent in the Benedictine Priory at Hereford. Three days before he left on a trip to France with Basil Poutiatine, Hopkins wrote on July 7, 1867 to E. W. Urquhart: "I am hoping to go to Paris with Poutiatine next week but at present I am in the position of writing letters to him which I believe he never gets. After a week or ten days I return. I have no plans till some time in August, when Pater is going to ask me down to Sidmouth."[26] Pater often spent his summer holidays abroad, away from the quiet pensiveness of Oxford. However when he did remain in England, he frequently invited some of his pupils to share some of his vacation. In his memories of Pater at Brasenose, T. H. Ward remembered a pleasant month he spent at Sidmouth with Pater which "made us intimate, and afterwards I often

walked and lunched with Pater at Oxford."[27] Gosse remembered
Pater as very gracious and affable, while others, though not
contradicting him, remark that they never really knew just how
much Pater was with them. A. C. Benson thought that Pater's
asking students to join him in vacation was a ". . . severe tax
on one so independent and fond of seclusion as Pater. . . . At
the same time, says one of those who came within his circle in
later days, it was felt that his relations with younger men were
guided more by a sense of duty than by instinct."[28] So when
Hopkins noted in a letter on August 15, 1867, to Urquhart after
he got back from France, "Pater has not written,"[29] it is less
important that the invitation never came through than that
Pater had him in mind for a vacation visit. It ought to be remembered that Hopkins had been a Catholic since October 21, 1866.

In the autumn of 1867, Hopkins went to Newman's Oratory
to teach. It was an arduous period for him. Teaching duties
enervated him and tensions over the possibility of his having a
religious vocation distracted him. He left to go into a retreat in
the full sense of the expression during Holy Week, April 5,
1868. His retreat master was a Jesuit, Father Henry James
Coleridge, who some years later as the editor of *The Month*
rejected Hopkins' ode, "The Wreck of the Deutschland." The
retreat apparently encouraged his religious vocation, for he left
the Oratory permanently on April 15, and on April 27 he made
another retreat at the Jesuit novitiate at Roehampton. On May
6, he was home, resolved to be a priest, but still unsure whether
to be a Benedictine or a Jesuit. Sometime between May 6 and
May 11, he decided on the Jesuits, for on the latter fateful day
he burned his poems.[30] In several senses, on this day he started
a fire which never went out. On May 19, he saw the Very
Reverend Alfred Weld, Provincial of the English Province of
the Society of Jesus, to petition to be received into the Society.
He was accepted on May 30, 1868.

Two days before his reception, Hopkins went to Oxford. On
May 29 he took his degree. "—Saw Swinburne. Met Mr. Solomon," he recorded.[31] Swinburne and Simeon Solomon were
members of a circle of painters and writers who espoused Theo-
phile Gautier's "art for art's sake" program for the modern school

in which Gautier made the sole purpose of art the attainment
of aesthetic perfection of the absolutely beautiful thing. The
group[32] included John Payne, Arthur O'Shaughnessy, and J. T.
Nettleship. Swinburne was its outstanding member, for his
"algolagnic blues" were raising temperatures in the aesthetic
hothouses in England with their exotic French growths. Solomon
was a disciple of the Pre-Raphaelites at first and, painting in
their manner, he achieved note. Then he adopted what might
be called the pagan manner which merited him mention in
Robert Buchanan's article, "The Fleshly School of Poetry," in
the *Contemporary Review*. An acquaintance of Pater's, Swinburne often visited Oxford, and very likely, it was through
Swinburne that Pater met Solomon whose work was quite popular
in Oxford during the 1860's as was the painter himself.[33]

Hopkins was ever interested in painting. He even considered
becoming a painter himself except he felt it might endanger his
moral life. His favorite painter was Millais who he thought the
greatest of English painters and one of the world's greats. It is
not thus surprising to see the entry for June 17, 1868, in his
Journal: "Fine. To lunch with Pater, then to Mr. Solomon's
studio and the Academy."[34] He then lists some of the works he
saw, among them some Millais. This was one of his summer
pleasures before he was to enter the Jesuit novitiate. Some of
the others were a concert, visiting friends and relatives, and a
trip with Edward Bond to Switzerland. Throughout all of this
is Hopkins' ever-present agile eye whose delicate sensitivities
continue to be recorded in his letters and his journals. The importance of all this is that the decision on his vocation did not
make him change his friends or his interests—at least not at
first.

On September 7, 1868, Hopkins went to Roehampton to the
Jesuit novitiate. He knew his going would cut him off from the
world, and he was quite prepared that this should be so. The
generosity that went into his choice is particularly evident in the
turmoil of his "Slaughter of the innocents," whose full meaning
lies hidden in the calm report to Bridges three months later:
"I cannot send my *Summa* for it is burnt with my other verses:
I saw they would interfere with my state and vocation."[35] That

sense of leaving the world is made sharply apparent to the
Jesuit novice, for shortly after his admittance he begins the Long
Retreat—thirty days of Spiritual Exercises of St. Ignatius.

Hopkins' main thoughts for two years were his prayers. Then
he began his academic studies for the priesthood in September
of 1870, the first phase of which—philosophy—ended on June
23, 1873. The most notable event of this time of his life was his
discovery of the philosophy of Scotus. The rest was watching
and receiving. Theology began, after a year of teaching rhetoric
at Roehampton, in August, 1874, with ordination coming three
years later. As his priestly preparation neared those last stages
after which he was to go back into the world, his poetic vigor,
"That fine delight . . . ," revived after ten years, a presage of
his true personality. It is not surprising that his ode, "The Wreck
of the Deutschland," is primarily about his own solitudes of soul
and that the shipwreck in the outside world is made to answer
to his experiences. This first great modern poem shows that it
was a poet who went into retreat.

Though Hopkins had some contacts with his friends—Baillie
and Bridges for example—through infrequent visits and letters,
during his priestly preparation, he was out of sight. So it is not
surprising that after his ordination, his old interests and associates are picked up again. Even before his ordination, they are
in evidence. Despite long and careful preparation for his final
examinations in theology, he wrote a long letter to Robert Bridges
filled with literary interests: critiques of Bridges' own poetry,
general remarks on poetic rhythms, especially Milton's, and
most interestingly, a passage which indicates that Hopkins was
quite abreast of current literary vogues out in the world of
letters: "Crying up great names, as for instance the reviews do
now Swinburne and Hugo, those plagues of mankind, is often
wicked and in general is a great vanity and full of impious brag
and a blackguard and unspiritual mind."[36]

Did Hopkins associate ". . . a blackguard and unspiritual
mind" with the one man others were identifying as the source
of such "plagues," Walter Pater and his *Studies in the History
of the Renaissance* with its famous philosophy of the passionate
imagination in its "Conclusion?" It is important to remember

how comfortable this identity was before considering Hopkins' attitude towards Pater.

There was in formation in the middle part of the century a state of mind which was to reach its zenith in the 1890's, which because of its myriad sources and personalities, has been given the general designation, "fin de siècle," in its terminal stages. As to the sources, there are Gautier and the French Symbolists, Ruskin's *Modern Painters,* and the general decay of the spiritual sense in English culture coupled with what Arnold saw as the tedium of the modern age—smug vulgarity. There was a distemper in the air which in its artistic implications provided us with a bizarre lot of personalities who succeeded in alienating most of the Victorian respectables by combining paganism, sex, and religion as the main excitations of their interests and efforts. Mention has already been made of one coterie around Swinburne. Earlier and more significant were the Pre-Raphaelites headed by Rossetti; later and less significant was the Rhymers' Club whose greatest distinction is that Yeats passed by. Graham Hough summarized this movement:

We are faced with the history of an immense number of explorations, many false starts and blind alleys, and not a few personal tragedies, all directed to finding some sort of accommodation between art and a bourgeois society. This involved many experiments, in ethics, aesthetics, poetical and artistic technique. No English or French writer of this movement can be said to have solved his problem, or ended in an Olympian calm; and we shall hardly find it possible to record any final messages of ripe wisdom."[37]

In the middle of this chaotic spirit came the publication of *Renaissance.* To Pater's surprise, his book was being taken as the "revealed word" of this movement. Not only did the disciples hail this revelation, but as A. C. Benson noted: "Young men with vehement impulses, with no experience of the world, no idea of the solid impenetrable weight of social traditions and prejudices, found in the principles enunciated by Pater with so much recondite beauty, so much magical charm, a new equation of values."[38] Pater, shocked at the possibility of his book being misleading especially to the young, suppressed the "Conclusion"

in the second edition of the *Renaissance* in 1877, and did not
publish another book for twelve years. Still his name and words
became preacher and sermon among the new aesthetes.

One kind of reaction to all of this that is more imaginative
than the usual adult response—strictures—is youthful in spirit—
parody. This is exactly what William H. Mallock, an Oxford
undergraduate, did by writing a satire on the world he was
preparing to enter. He made a menagerie of the notables of his
day, put them talking in their characteristic styles on their
favorite topics with appropriate caricatural touches, and thus
produced a highly amusing book, *The New Republic: or, Culture, Faith, and Philosophy in an English Country House.*
Mallock wrote to Thomas Wright: "The fanciful sketch of Pater
introduced into *The New Republic* was meant to represent an
attitude of mind rather than a man," but Wright comments that
the portrait is faithful to the man. According to Wright, most
of Mallock's impressions were secondhand.[39]

There is no question that Mallock caught Pater's mode of
mind though he, perhaps, substituted for Pater's speech those
soft undulating qualities of his prose style. Here Mr. Rose, the
aesthete, reveals himself to his guests for the first time: " 'To
me,' he said, raising his eyebrows wearily, and sending his words
floating down the table in a languid monotone, '. . . I rather
look upon life as a chamber, which we decorate as we would
decorate the chamber of woman or youth that we love, tinting
the walls of it with symphonies of subdued colour, and filling
it with works of fair form, and with flowers, and with strange
scents, and with the instruments of music.' "[40] Or when the
conversation touches upon culture as the aim of life, Mr. Rose
rhapsodizes: " 'Or sometimes,' said Mr. Rose dreamily, as if his
talk was lapsing into a soliloquy, 'when he is a mere passing
observer of things, letting impressions from without move him
as they will, I would compare the man to an Aeolian harp,
which the winds at will play through—a beautiful face, a rainbow, a ruined temple, a death-bed, or a line of poetry, wandering in like a breath of air amongst the chords of his soul, touching note after note into soft music, and at last gently dying away
into silence.' "[41]

The satiric design in Mallock's *New Republic* is to show the heterodoxy of the times to be intellectually vapid, ethically fatuous, culturally sterile, and religiously damning. This was Mallock's own response to Oxford as an undergraduate and to the modern intelligentsia at large in his maturity. All his life, he tilted at the way the world was going—to religious liberalism and scientific optimism. *The New Republic* is actually a series of dialogues on the decline of civilization put in the mouths of those principals who were, in Mallock's judgment, presiding over its downfall: Arnold, Pater, Huxley, Tyndall, and Jowett together with some lesser lights and social types. As Mr. Herbert (a vague replica of Ruskin who was the one eminent Victorian Mallock could respect) remarked, " 'The whole human race,' he went on in measured melancholy accents, 'is now wandering in an accursed wilderness, which not only shows us no hilltop whence the promised land may be seen, but which, to most of the wanderers, seems a promised land itself. And they have a God of their own too, who engages now to lead them out of it if they will only follow him: who, for visible token of his Godhead, leads them with a pillar of cloud by day, and a pillar of fire by night—the cloud being the black smoke of their factory chimneys, and the fire the red glare of their blast-furnaces. And so effectual are these modern, divine guides, that if we were standing on the brink of Jordan itself, we should be utterly unable to catch, through the fire and the smoke, one single glimpse of the sunlit hills beyond.' "[42]

To Mallock, Pater represented the degradation of the arts in that time. Mallock saw in Pater's approach to art the kind of aestheticism which, despite all of its charming, ethereal flights, would lead to low, sensual titillations. So while he mimics the impressionistic flights, he is really suggesting the covert voluptuary. The quality which really stands out in all of Mr. Rose's passages is a kind of sycophant salaciousness. This is evident in all the passages of Mr. Rose which substantially reveal his temper of personality and it always accompanies his attitudes. Mr. Rose, in his first important speech, says, " 'We have learned that the aim of life is life; and what does successful life consist in? Simply,' said Mr. Rose, speaking very slowly, and with a soft solemnity, 'in the consciousness of exquisite living—in the making our own each highest thrill of joy that the moment offers us—be it some touch of colour on the sea or on the mountains, the early dew in the crimson shadows of a rose, the shining of a woman's limbs in clear water, or—' " As if the passage itself would not be enough for the effect intended, Mallock has Mr. Rose interrupted by the very embarrassment of the group: "Here unfortunately a sound of 'Sh' broke softly from several mouths."[43] What Mallock has done is to transpose satirically the "Conclusion" of the Renaissance into a point of view, a manner of expression, and a not so subtle implication. The pointed result is to surround the figure of Mr. Rose continually with a low level of interest disguised as aesthetic sophistication and thus convict the Paterian spirit on two levels: hypocrisy and sexual disequilibrium.

Decadence is indelicately stamped on all of Mr. Rose's conversations whether as statements of attitudes or verbalizations of those very feelings. In his next speech, Mr. Rose says, " 'I . . . look upon social dissolution as the true condition of the most perfect life. For the centre of life is the individual, and it is only through dissolution that the individual can re-emerge.' " This dissolution sometimes takes on a morbidity, as in one of two long and central passages in Book III, Chapter 2, in which Mr. Rose expostulates on the aim of culture which " ' . . . is indeed to make the soul a musical instrument . . . ,' " and ends by his relating a walk he took between Charing Cross and Westminster as a kind of imaginative levitation, " '. . . hoping I might see some unfortunate cast herself from the Bridge of Sighs. It was a night well in harmony with despair. Fancy . . . the infinity of emotions which the sad and sudden splash in the dark river would awaken in one's mind—and all due to that one poem of Hood's.' "[44]

In what are perhaps the main passages Mallock gives to Mr. Rose (in Book IV, Chapter 1), the satirist strikes at the insidious eclecticism he saw in Pater, especially the relating of pagan and Christian values through the medium of eroticism. It all begins with Mr. Rose, who takes it upon himself to explain the tendencies and directions to which his tastes lead. Mr. Rose explains the necessity of what might be called the exclusively aesthetic taste; he sees an increase in the kind of men " '. . . who with a steady and set purpose follow art for the sake of art, beauty for the sake of beauty, love for the sake of love, life for the sake of life.' " This is, of course, a grossly simplified version of a passage from the "Conclusion," but it sets up the satirical snare, for antipathetic contents of such experiences, according to Mallock, are shockingly juxtaposed as compatibly contributory to the best experience of art, beauty, love, and life. This takes the form of Mr. Rose's discourses on architecture, painting, and poetry as they might become in an utopian London under his inspiration. Having started by suggesting that though his vision may seem dreamlike, he offers the possibility of realization of a London of aesthetic exquisiteness: " '. . . it is quite conceivable that we might some day have a capital, the entire aspect of which should be the visible embodiment of our finest and most varied culture, our most sensitive taste, and our deepest aesthetic measure of things.' "[45] He mentions the names Romano, Vasari, and Campi as the inspirations for the streets, galleries, houses, and theaters; Ghiberti and Michelangelo would be taken as the models for the metalwork; and indeed the pavements would rival Domenico Beccafumi! The eclectic spirit of this taste is best expressed in the statuary. In place of vulgar advertisements: "They [feelings] will rest instead, here on an exquisite fountain, here on a statue, here on a bust of Zeus or Hermes or Aphrodite, glimmering in a laurelled nook; or on a *Mater Dolorosa* looking down on you from her holy shrine. . . .' " Continuing in the vein of " 'no style in particular, but a *renaissance* of all styles,' " Mr. Rose says, " 'It will matter nothing to us whether they be pagan or Catholic, classical or medieval. We shall be quite without prejudice or bigotry. To the eye of true taste, an Aquinas in his cell before a crucifix, or a Narcissus gazing at himself in a still fountain, are—in their own ways, you know—equally beautiful.' "[46] To hold the notion that these are "equally beautiful" apart from Truth is an unconscionable attitude in Mallock's view, a view which he cleverly expresses by having the only Roman Catholic in the group, Miss Merton (who is based upon Mallock's cousin Isey, daughter of William Froude, later **Baroness**

A. von Hugel), object to considering St. Thomas out of his
Christian context by quoting from Newman's "Dream of Geron-
tius." This makes Mr. Rose think of devils, and he recalls that
only Milton's had any taste. This causes Mr. Saunders (a sketchy
version of William Kingdon Clifford, the mathematician), a
blustering materialist, to remark, " 'Dante's biggest devil . . .
chewed Judas Iscariot like a quid of tobacco, to all eternity.
He, at any rate, knew what he liked.' " Having rendered heaven's
judgment on the aesthete, Mallock gives him another knock by
showing his reaction as being one of inane indifference. "Mr.
Rose started, and visited Mr. Saunders with a rapid frown. He
then proceeded, turning to Miss Merton as if nothing had
happened."[47]

Mr. Rose proceeds to poetry, which is the way the satirist
brings up Pater's interest in Catholic ritual. Again he suggests
that something is amiss, for this interest is held by a man really
skeptical of the Christian religion (the early Pater). Moreover,
he misuses religious ritual for aesthetic ends which, it must be
remembered according to Mallock, are shams for base eroticism.
This depiction begins by Mr. Rose reading "a nice sonnet" to
the group. The sonnet bears repeating here:

> "Three visions in the watches of the night.
> Made sweet my sleep—almost too sweet to tell.
> One was Narcissus by a woodside well,
> And on the moss his limbs and feet were white;
> And one, Queen Venus, blown for my delight
> Across the blue sea in a rosy shell;
> And one, a lean Aquinas in his cell,
> Kneeling, his pen in hand, with aching sight
> Strained towards a carven Christ; and of these three
> I knew not which was fairest. First I turned
> Towards that soft boy, who laughed and fled from me;
> Towards Venus then; and she smiled once, and she
> Fled also. Then with teeming heart I yearned,
> O Angel of the Schools, towards Christ with thee!"[48]

As we read this today, there is a remarkable augury in this poem
that works very much against its satiric intent, which is the
erogenous abomination of modern aestheticism. The marks of

this are quite clear within the poem. In fact, the sonnet is really a kind of poetic celebration of this theme, the makings of which begin to be provided from Mr. Rose's first appearance and are shown to be the main personal characteristic of the aesthete, namely, prurience. It will be remembered that Mr. Rose talks about decorating "the chamber of the woman or youth we love" in his first appearance. The next manifestation he talks about are the values of "social dissolution," followed later by one kind of example—"a beautiful face, a rainbow, a ruined temple, a death-bed, or a line of poetry. . . ." Then comes this grand enactment in Book IV capped with its sonnet " 'written by a boy of eighteen—a youth of extraordinary promise, I think, whose education I may myself claim to have had some share in directing.' " There may be here implied more than just self-corruption. And as if he had not made all the worst possibilities evidently clear, Mallock goes on to the association with Catholic ritual, whose unmistakable identification with Pater raises the question of the moral probity of his satire. Finally, Mr. Rose tries to make his idea of true religion and culture clearer in its historic patterns: " 'I often figure to myself an unconscious period and a conscious period, as two women—one an untamed creature with embrowned limbs native to the air and the sea; the other marblewhite and swan-soft, couched delicately on cushions before a mirror, and watching her own supple reflection gleaming in the depths of it.' "[49] He goes on in such a vein, ending by saying of the second of the two women, " 'There is a sadness—a languor, even in the grave tendrils of her heavy hair, and in each changing curve of her bosom as she breathes or sighs.' " Mallock has Lady Ambrose loudly whisper the point: " 'What a very odd man Mr. Rose is! . . . He always seems to talk of everybody as if they had no clothes on.' " Undaunted, Mr. Rose goes on finally to: " 'Such a woman do I see whenever I enter a ritualistic church—' "[50] Unsurprisingly, the last we see of Mr. Rose, he is trying to purchase a pornographic book for which he makes an outlandish offer (Mallock upped the offer from twenty-five pounds to thirty after his first [*Belgravia*] edition).[51]

The New Republic was a popular success, for it went through some nine editions before 1910 and at least one edition every year from 1877 through 1881. This is not counting its first publication in magazine form. The result was that it gave to Pater a notoriety beyond anything brought to him by his writings to that time. To the general intelligentsia, he was Mr. Rose. A. C. Benson judged the association unjust: "Pater had indeed laid himself in one sense open to the attack, by committing to the impersonal medium of a book sentiments which could be distorted into the sensuous creed of aesthetes; to satirize the advanced type of the aesthetic school was perfectly fair, but it was unduly harsh to cause an affected and almost licentious extravagance of behaviour to be attributed to one whose private life and conversation were of so sober and simple a character." Ferris Greenslet generally agrees. Thomas Wright disagrees; he quotes an acquaintance of Pater's attesting to the "truth as to one side of Pater's nature."[52]

The personal effect on Pater of Mallock's perverse picture of him is ambiguously reported. Benson wrote: "It seems clear that the satire caused Pater considerable distress. If he had been personally vain or socially ambitious, it might have gratified him to be included in so distinguished a company; but all this was entirely foreign to his retired and studious habits; he did not at all desire to have a mysterious and somewhat painful prestige thrust upon him; and though he seldom if ever spoke of the subject to his most intimate friends, yet it is impossible not to realize that the satire must have caused him sincere pain."[53] In contrast, Wright states, ". . . we are able to declare positively that, instead of suffering distress, he took it as a compliment, thoroughly enjoyed it and laughed heartily at the passages that went nearest the truth. Pater was troubled, indeed, not because people might recognize the portrait, but because he feared that they might not recognize it."[54] Edmund Gosse, who came to know Pater before *The New Republic* portrait, wrote that Pater thought his portrait "a little unscrupulous," that some of its details were disconcerting, but that he admired "the cleverness and promise of the book, and it did not cause him to alter his mode of life or thought in the smallest degree." Gosse says that Pater was even flattered and complimented to be put in such company. "What he liked less, what did really ruffle him, was the persistence with which the newspapers at this time began to attribute to him all sorts of 'aesthetic' follies and extravagances. He said to me, in 1876: 'I wish they wouldn't call me 'a hedonist'; it produces such a bad effect on the minds of people who don't know Greek.'" Gosse then notes that this led to the suppression of the "Conclusion" in the second edition of Pater's *Renaissance*.[55]

The distinguished professor of Greek at Balliol, Benjamin Jowett, was neither complimented nor flattered to be associated with the modern Pagans. Already alarmed by Pater's *Renaissance*, this most powerful figure in the University now saw its author publicly affiliated with coteries shockingly alien (to which he was indifferent) to himself and to Oxford. Besides, as Iain Fletcher wrote, "Neither in his gifts, nor in his eccentricities, was Pater a typical Oxford man. He was not an exact scholar; he was not in large companies a ready or amusing talker. He owed his Fellowship partly to his gifts as a stylist, but even his style was not in the main Victorian tradition of Oxford prose."[56] The upshot of this seems to have been Pater's not being given university appointments, and it is generally thought that this was Jowett's doing.[57]

To return now to the question proposed: Did Hopkins accept Mr. Rose as the authentic Pater, and thus find it necessary, however reluctantly, to avoid any association with his friend? Pater's antipathy to Christianity was one thing, but now a public reputation for a wicked hedonism was something else indeed. There is no doubt that Hopkins knew Mallock's satire. In a letter to his mother he described a Sir Gore Ouseley who came up to Oxford to lecture on organ music: "Sir Gore (ghastly as this is, what else can you say?—his name in a book of Mallock's would become Sir Bloodclot Reekswell). . . ."[58] In another letter, this to Bridges, he complimented his friend for not writing poems which are merely vowel sounds arranged ". . . as Mallock says, very thinly costuming a strain of conventional passion, kept up by stimulants, and crying always in a high head voice about flesh and flowers and democracy and damnation."[59]

While it may be safely said that Hopkins shared with Mallock in good measure the same demurs about the way the modern

world was going, he continued to be friendly with Pater, associated with him when possible, and was pleased to hear of
Pater's regard. Using Hopkins' other friendships as models, this
is tantamount to saying that throughout his lifetime, Hopkins
had an affection for Pater. The evidence for this judgment is not
rife, but what there is—considered in the context of the "Conclusion," Mallock, Jowett, Swinburne, and the newspapers—
convincingly suggests the soundness of such an opinion. Moreover, nothing has ever been turned up to show that Hopkins in
any way joined in any attack upon Pater or his writings.

Most of the evidence importantly occurs soon after Hopkins'
ordination when, in the first fervor of his priestly vocation, he
was setting out to begin what he hoped would be a long and
fruitful service, and when Pater's notorious caricature was becoming popular through Mallock's satire. Yet Hopkins wrote on
April 2, 1878, to Bridges from Mount St. Mary's College, Ches-
terfield, his first assignment: "It was pleasing and flattering to
hear that Mr. Pater remembers and takes an interest in me."[60]
After an unsuccessful summer preaching stint at the Jesuit Mount
Street Church (the personal significance of this is taken up in
the next chapter), Hopkins was eventually assigned to St.
Aloysius' Church, Oxford. In a postcard of December 9, 1878
to Bridges telling him of his new station, Hopkins wrote: "More
of my acquaintances are up than I thought would be. I have
seen Pater."[61] To his mother two months later, he mentioned:
"I went yesterday to dine with the Paters."[62] That was February.
In May he had Pater to dine with him as Pater's note in the
Bodleian shows. Moreover, Hopkins later wrote his friend,
Baillie, that though he liked both the Town and Gown, he saw
little of the university, that he felt "alien," "chilling," and "dis-
trusted." He said he might have wished to have been unknown
there even though some whom he saw were friendly and cordial;
but ". . . with others I could not feel at home." In light of this,
Hopkins' association with Pater takes on even more significance.

It would be an error to consider Hopkins' friendship for Pater
simply a work of apostolic charity. Hopkins saw a good deal of
Pater while he was at St. Aloysius, not because it was most con-
venient to spend time with a former mentor and now an in-

fluential literary personality, but because both men had artistic personalities which they found to be highly compatible to each other. Staid Catholic Hopkinsians of the literary apologete variety will bristle at this, but all the evidence is against them. The slur they take this to be against Hopkins is indeed a slur, though of their own making, for such an attitude takes away from Hopkins his good sense, objectivity, and equipoise in distinguishing between the Pater he knew as an undergraduate and the Mr. Rose of the pursed-lipped intelligentsia. Of course, there was the chance that the young don of Brasenose had let his delicate sensitivities slip into something abhorrent. The "Conclusion" could be read that way. However, limited to the experience of art and stressing the ideal mode of perception as the uncloyed senses, Pater could be calling characteristically for the pure moment of art, which is to say, the sensuous apprehension and the emotive response heightened to the point of spiritualization. This could be what the *Renaissance* demonstrates and the "Conclusion" exhortatively explains. This need not have been a new Pater to Hopkins, but rather a more dynamically graphic one emerging—Ruskin got up in fancier clothes.

There is every reason to believe that undergraduate Hopkins found in Pater a most engaging person whose latent attitudes on life, art, and religion were quietly evocative and interesting; now returned to Oxford, Father Hopkins renewed his friendship at a time when Pater's views had advanced to stages wherein their main tendencies had been more elaborately demonstrated and impressively stated. Even so, much of the intelligent public misunderstood the implications of Pater's mind. Moreover, there was, for the cruder sort, fun as well as the satisfactions of moral indignation. Father Hopkins, while in Oxford, saw behind the public flippancy and parasitical dilettantism to a Pater who was genuine in character, genial in company; an artist whose style evinced a most extraordinary insight into the mind and heart of artistic beauty. (By contrast, Jowett did not see the true Pater until the very end.) That something like this must be the case follows from the quality of person that G. M. Hopkins was. Were there even a trace of the hedonic aesthete in Pater, this line would very likely have never occurred in that letter of

Hopkins (written after he was dispatched to serve in Liverpool) to his long-time friend, A. W. M. Baillie about his sojourn at Oxford: "By the by when I was at Oxford Pater was one of the men I saw most of."[63]

It is likely that the vagaries of Hopkins' career prevented his friendship with Pater from being a continuously close one. Moreover, Pater—unlike Hopkins—was not a letter writer. There was probably a falling off due to time and distance, but there is no evidence of a falling out. We can imagine the kind of letters the two might have exchanged; even more happily, something more than inferences would be left us about their states of mind. What did happen was that each went his separate way. In each case, that way was in large measure shut off from the world, for both men had Platonic personalities: their essential selves seemed shrouded by quiet, darkening social attributes. Both gave those around them a sense of a more substantive life buried beneath a sweet and easy manner. Pater and Hopkins were elusive men to sense and know, perhaps because of the extent of their human dimensions, their capacities to project the fullness of their senses and feelings through and behind powerfully empathic styles—masks of artifice. Hopkins remained more hidden than Pater, for so far as we know, Pater never saw a line of his poetry. However Pater published *Marius The Epicurean* in 1885 and *Imaginary Portraits* in 1887. Given Hopkins' enormous interest in letters, it is unthinkable that he did not know them. Still there is no extant evidence that he did. Both works would have interested him; *Marius* would have drawn his special attention with its religious implications of which he knew a great deal from the author's side. Of course, these were Hopkins' Dublin years. Pater may have been one of those roots that got no rain.

There is a bit of a chance that Hopkins and Pater did not completely lose touch after the second spell of their Oxford days. Hopkins was back at St. Aloysius' Church, St. Giles', Oxford on September 11, 1883, but only briefly. However, on a trip from Dublin he stopped at Oxford on May 4, 1886 for what seems a longer period. He saw some of his Oxford friends, the Paravicinis family for example. He had a short trip to see Bridges and meet his wife.[64] It is not impossible to suppose that he made an effort to see Pater, one of the few at the university who had remained friendly. He had been gone since February 1884, and it is possible that he had not seen Pater since serving at St. Aloysius. Pater usually spent term-time at Brasenose. However, he made no mention of it in his letters of the time.

So much for the extant biographical evidence of the Hopkins-Pater friendship. While the evidence is thin, what there is is quite sufficient to substantiate the impression that they were friends. It has been found that what began as an undergraduate academic relationship grew into a cordial friendship which reached its greatest intimacy during the period in which Hopkins was stationed in Pater's home base, Oxford. The biographical facts clearly show that Hopkins and Pater saw each other frequently during this time and that they got on well despite the fact that it was now Father Hopkins of the Society of Jesus and that Pater was being called Mr. Rose. Hopkins' assignments which took him away from Oxford and eventually as far as Dublin caused their associations to be infrequent though there is no evidence that their relation suffered any serious break. There is the scrap of evidence that Hopkins might have seen Pater at least once after being assigned to Ireland. To Pater's missive lethargy must be added Hopkins' illnesses in Ireland—all of which goes a long way to explain the gap of information in the 1880's. Finally, there is no evidence whatsoever either from Hopkins or Pater of any loss of affection for each other.

IV

I have suggested that Hopkins knew full well how much of a caricature of Pater Mallock's Mr. Rose was and thus how wrongheaded was public opinion. My attitude, however, is not based solely on Hopkins' moral integrity; it is also based on Pater's. By suppressing his "Conclusion," Pater must have chased any lingering doubt, if there was any in the first place, from Hopkins' mind about the wholesomeness of the views in the *Renaissance.* Too much cannot be made of how this would have impressed Hopkins for both moral as well as personal reasons. To begin with the personal, it ought to be remembered that such an act is the most salient issue in Hopkins' life, a fact that will be gone into in some detail later on. Hopkins knew the agony of sacrificing one's work; the sort of character demanded to do such a thing came of an intense and weary experience, the kind that brings an absolute awareness: this he knew personally. So Pater's decision to suppress the "Conclusion" most surely would have confirmed Hopkins' respect for Pater. Moreover, Pater's stated reason for his action displayed the kind of judgment which Hopkins would have admired. Pater wrote: "This brief 'Conclusion' was omitted in the second edition of this book, as I conceived it might possibly mislead some of those young men into whose hands it might fall. On the whole, I have thought it best to reprint it here, with some slight changes which bring it closer to my original meaning."[65] This is a note he wrote for his collected works regarding this controversial essay. What is significant is his moral sensitivity. When the "Conclusion" first appeared, it was misinterpreted in such a way that it could do moral harm to young people aspiring to the arts. In addition, it was being quoted as the oracle of deviant persons of various kinds whose true purposes were hardly the cultivation of the arts. The fundamental error was considering what he had written apart from a moral system. This is what he meant in the last line of his note: "I have dealt more fully in *Marius The Epicurean* with the thoughts suggested by it." In other words, *Marius* provided the moral side of his philosophy of art, thereby giving a proper context for the "Conclusion."

There is further evidence for the quality of Pater's moral sensitivity regarding the influence of books.[66] In a letter to Oscar Browning, a Cambridge friend, Pater baldly states that he did not share Browning's amusement over parental concern about Pater's alleged recommendation and loan to a young Eton boy of a copy of *Mademoiselle de Maupin*. Pater wrote that he would strongly oppose the book's being lent to any young person, or even its being around them. He noted that he could not recommend it to anybody. He asked that "unqualified denial" be made to the parties concerned. Such remarks, he wrote, were misrepresentative as well as deeply painful. This letter was probably written after the initial critical reactions to the *Renaissance*, and perhaps after Pater's failing to achieve the university proctorship.

It would be a mistake to attribute this care merely to pride and ambition. Pater always understood art to have a certain moral tone, and he was extremely sensitive in his own writing to this aspect of the public's response to his work. Sixteen years after the letter about Gautier's novel, Pater rushed to see Lionel Johnson concerning his review of his new book, *Appreciations,* a review which had appeared in a journal entitled *The Century Guild Hobby Horse.* Apparently, Pater was considerably worried over being depicted as a rampant aesthete. To his pleasure, he found Johnson's article to be "careful and scholarly." However, *Appreciations* did not generally receive such a pleasant reception. Pater had included in the first edition an early essay (1868) entitled, "Aesthetic Poetry." It especially received unfavorable notice despite its modifications from an earlier version. He struck it out of the second edition because of the possibility of some offense against piety. Eventually, he omitted it from his collected works.

Furthermore, he was just as forthright about the work of his former students and acquaintances. He advised Arthur Symons, for example, to omit an offensive poem from his forthcoming volume and to make revisions in another. He specifically objected to the frequent use of Christ's name in these poems in ways defaulting good taste. It is significant that Symons, one of the young leaders of the aesthetic movement in England, for the most part ignored his former mentor's advice.

When George Moore sent his *Confessions of a Young Man* to him, Pater acknowledged the gift along with some politely appreciative but pungent demurs. He told Moore that he disagreed with him on a good many things. He quoted *Hamlet:* "Thou com'st in such a questionable shape!" as his response to Moore's book, and said he meant moral "shape." Finally, he offered Moore the speculation that he was missing a good deal of life by his narrow, vituperative, "cynical" look at the world, however zestful and vivid his spirit.

There is, then, good reason to uphold Pater's artistic integrity.

Always aware of the moral element in the quality of the arts, Pater seems to have developed this sensitivity more and more until it became a substantive part of his view. On his own work or with that of others, he exercised a most assiduous concern for moral respect and good taste. Perhaps this is easier said about others than done to one's own work. Hard as it is to apply a code personally, Pater manifested his greatest care on his own efforts. And when he erred in his judgment, he quickly corrected his mistake. Indeed, even given Victorian sensibility, Pater seemed scrupulous in these matters. Nevertheless, as his letters to his publisher, Alexander Macmillan, reveal, Pater had a great solicitude for every detail of his literary offerings to the public. He would not have seemed so scrupulous to Hopkins, of course, who was much more acute than Pater. What is important is the basis of mutual respect in each other's views.

There is no need to leave Hopkins' attitude in conjecture, though the burning of his own works and their general suppression all his life is more than enough warrant to say that Hopkins knew the sorrow and loss of such destruction. I refer to the famous episode between Hopkins and Coventry Patmore in which Hopkins' hesitations over a much loved and labored upon prose work of Patmore's—*Sponsa Dei*—was a contributing factor to Patmore's burning his work. Hopkins wrote Patmore after hearing of his action: "Your news was that you had burnt the book called *Sponsa Dei*, and that on reflection upon remarks of mine. I wish I had been more guarded in making them. When we take a step like this we are forced to condemn ourselves: either our work should never have been done or never undone, and either way our time and toil are wasted—a sad thought; though the intention may at both times have been good." It is clear that the enormous personal significance of such actions was painfully acute to Hopkins; so is the suasion of the commanding principle of conscience.

And it is the principle behind the pain that is so meaningful here, the principle that justifies the sacrifice. This principle is: Art is made for man. Implicit in this axiom is the value judgment that good art enhances human nature so that the array of human powers and their possibilities are developed, enlarged towards their more perfect fulfillment through the instrumentality of the artifice. The difficulty is in the converse of this notion, making the practical judgment in the case of a specific work of art, especially one's own. Here the artist confronts society either as a benefactor or a malefactor in the ethical abstract, but within the creative personality of the artist, the real circumstances of his prudence, the judgmental struggle has its analogies to suicide. As Hopkins wrote, "When we take a step like this we are forced to condemn ourselves. . . ."[67] Yet such an action is the most decisive way of specifying the role of art in life, for at these times the high intention is to make art serve man, its creator. Of course, this is precisely what the aesthetes were against; it is what "art for art's sake" meant.

It is commonplace today to hear that books do not have the kind of radical influence upon readers that this attitude presumes, a view endemic to an age of literary vulgarity in which so many books have no kind of influence at all. It nevertheless is a fact that writers like Pater, Patmore, and Hopkins thought differently. Pater very probably had Oxford students in mind. G. Tillotson thinks Oscar Wilde was a case in point. He had read the *Renaissance* as a freshman at Oxford and late in his life remarked that it had a "strange influence" on him. Tillotson thinks Pater saw in Wilde's *Dorian Gray* tangible evidence of a young man having been misled, for in reviewing this book Pater is quite candid on this point:

A true Epicureanism aims at a complete though harmonious development of man's entire organism. To lose the moral sense, therefore, for instance, the sense of sin and righteousness, as Mr. Wilde's hero—his heroes are bent on doing as speedily, as completely as they can, is to lose, or lower, organization, to become less complex, to pass from a higher to a lower degree of development.

Tillotson is no doubt right about Wilde being one of those Pater concerned himself about, though I think it is unfair to Pater to say that he spoke clearly too late.[68] He acted with the second edition of the *Renaissance*. I think Hopkins saw this in Pater's action, and along with the real possibilities at Oxford for clarifying exchanges on the differences between "experience" as Pater meant it as against "sensation" as the less perceptive thought he meant, he knew the real Pater behind the prose and prosaicism. By contrast, it took Jowett nearly Pater's whole lifetime to see the same.

The key issue on which to examine Hopkins and Pater is the good and the beautiful. Both held views in which these notions are strikingly similar, yet each approached them from different ways. Pater worked toward a moral system by way of art, and Hopkins sought art by way of a moral system. Historically, they seem to represent recapitulations of the Enlightenment, except art has replaced science as the "reasonable" way to faith (the good). While great intellectual interest lies in their attempted philosophical systems, surely the greatest significance lies in the way of life each system envisions beyond the frailty of time and mortality. This is what is enacted through their creative imaginations; however their systems fail, their art is a lasting monument to the glorious heights of their aspirations: "The fine delight . . ." and the ". . . gemlike flame. . . ."

CHAPTER III

Portraits in Silhouettes

THERE IS A REMARKABLE RESEMBLANCE between the literary lives of G. M. Hopkins and W. H. Pater. Perhaps the parallel has never been drawn because of the disproportion of evidence as well as interest. Hopkins has had his vogue in this century, which has added to his shelf, while Pater has remained a memory seldom remembered. Yet to the discerning eye there appears a distinct similarity in the literary malaise from which each suffered wearily for the whole of his life. Religion and art had disordering effects on both men. Though each chose to live according to one abiding interest—Hopkins for religion and Pater for art—the other like a ghost bidden was the secret sharer of their lives.

To picture their pain is no easy matter, for it was a special inner weariness which each bore as a latent but indelible mark. It did surface, of course, but being borne with such grace both within and without, it is most difficult to look behind the secret resolves of its bearers. We can, however, retrace the road each went; we can wonder what joys and sorrows each part of the journey brought; we can meditate on their works as the allegory of their lives. Thus perhaps we can come to understand how their restless spirits came through the glorious intercession of their words to a fulfilling paradox of peace.

I

Pater's "cry on the stair"

For the artist, the struggle is to create. Therein lies his main story, and while most often unknown, even the bare outlines are revealing. This struggle is often complicated by personal or professional matters or both. In Pater's case, this meant trying to maintain scholarly status at Oxford while satisfying his own aesthetic leanings by giving them some sort of expression. Considering what passes for university scholarship today, we would likely think that Pater's shelf would most certainly have brought him higher and higher university status. However, this was not the case, for the kind of scholarship valued at Oxford in Pater's day was Classical, factual, and textual. His *Studies in the History of the Renaissance*, his first major publication, did not bring his advancement despite its academic title. The reason is that it is a romantic, subjective, and aesthetic work. This is not to say that it has no scholarship, no historical sense, no objective grasp of the subject. It has all of these, perhaps in degrees hardly realized, but everything is made subservient to the subjective impulse of Pater's sculpted style. This seemed to link his book more with continental literary vagrancies than with the original and distinguished scholarship of a great university. The powers at Oxford thought this way and did not advance him in status.

The effect of this upon Pater must have been profound. To this was added an unsavory element in the public response to his book: the espousal of the "angry young men" of his day. They saw in the *Renaissance* the rationalization of all of their impulsive excesses and missed largely the meaning of the basic design. Pater had good reason to be downcast that so few understood the structure of the book. He had put it together with great care. At the outset, he had laid down the spirit of his inquiry, the bases for selection of his material, its historical range, and the judgmental means of determining its significance. To define in the most concrete terms the "special manifestation" of beauty, he wrote, was his aim. Judgment is made of two functions, he said: first, there is the personal sense of pleasure in a given object, the specification of the "sort or degree of pleasure," and the peculiar response it calls forth; secondly, there is the objectification of the pleasure by distinguishing, analyzing, and separating "from its adjuncts, the virtue by which a picture, a landscape, a fair personality in life or in a book, produces this special impression of beauty or pleasure, to indicate what the source of that impression is, and under what conditions it is experienced." Finally, Pater explained what he chose as the historical range of his study based on the unity he conceived the *Renaissance* of fifteenth-century Italy to have had—an "intimate alliance with mind," he called it.

When the body of the *Renaissance* is read in light of the plan in the Preface, providing that the style of the book is held in abeyance, the full realization of the design is evident. The first essay, "Two Early French Stories" shows according to Pater how far the *Renaissance* has its roots deep into the Middle Ages. Next an essay on Pico della Mirandola which stresses the coming together in the fifteenth century of the Greek and Christian religions. From the distillations of fifteenth-century Italian scholars, Pater moves to the center of his study by considering those men who, in his opinion, rendered through their art that rare unity of mind and feeling he thought so endemic to the time: Botticelli, Luca della Robbia, Michelangelo, Da Vinci, and (added in 1888) the Venetian school of Giorgione. The last two essays look ahead to the communication of this special spirit into a later time and place, in sixteenth-century France in the writings of Du Bellay and in early eighteenth-century Germany in the life of Johann Winckelmann. Finally, the famous "Conclusion," in which Pater so effectively stated the spirit of the aesthetic critic, cast in the flux of time, life, and art: fix your focus on each beautiful object and penetrate it for the fullest and highest moment it offers. This is what he had done in his study. He had "concluded" that his approach had wide merit on historical, critical, and aesthetic grounds.

The reception of his study brought to Pater sharp awareness of some vital realities about his work. First, he sadly found that the mode of this book, if followed in others, would not bring him advantages at Oxford. Moreover, some of his most deliberate touches had rebounded with false associations which seriously obscured the main tendencies of his mind and spirit. The question was how to go on plumbing the resources of his mind and spirit in ways which would be offered in formulations less open to misinterpretation, more covert in their personal implications, and clearly evidencing integrity of method and mind. Finally, there had surfaced in this book some hints of his deeper spiritual problems which would not be left submerged through literary camouflage simply because they pressed too vitally upon all his life and work. He had to deal with them, and that confrontation would heavily influence the shape of everything.

There was a twelve-year hiatus before Pater's next major book appeared. It has been standard to consider this period one of regret, dismay, and retreat. There is little question that these were aspects of this period, but too often they are offered as the characteristics of a defeated and inert personality. Nothing could be further from the truth. While the evidence of biographical import is meager about the whole of Pater's life, that fraction of the small number of letters Pater wrote, which are now extant, together with various unpublished manuscripts now available, afford sufficient evidence to obtain some accurate impression of Pater's literary plans.[1]

It must be remembered that by the middle of the 1870's Pater had established a place for himself in the world of letters. Despite certain unsatisfying elements, Pater's essays in *The Westminster Review* and the *Fortnightly Review* along with his *Renaissance* had attracted many to his style and not so many fewer to his mind. His publisher, Alexander Macmillan, had already published his first book and was eager for more. It is, therefore, not surprising to find that Pater did not quickly abandon this first mode of his work, but rather went on working on essays on subjects to which the bent of his spirit led him. We know that in March of 1877 he had determined on a new collection of essays upon which he had set to work.[2] The interests of these essays were to be more widely scattered. They were to consider Greek mythology, Venetian painting, and English literature, which is not surprising since the essays published up to this time had this range.

His proposal for a new book turned up in his letters to his publisher dealing with a new edition of his *Renaissance*. Macmillan had proposed a new edition in November, 1875, and Pater eagerly plunged into its preparation. He had a few minor revisions, he noted, along with some alterations to make this edition perfect. He again requested an engraved vignette which was to be put into the second edition and most subsequent ones—Da Vinci's "Head of a Youth." The most significant changes in this edition were his dropping of his "Conclusion," of the reworking of his essay on Wincklemann to make it less anti-Christian, and his adding to the first essay amplified in the second edition as the discussion of "Li Amitiez de Ami et Amile," with the new title, "Two Early French Stories." He also retitled the whole book, *The Renaissance, a Series of Studies in Art and Poetry, A New Edition.* It was published as *The Renaissance: Studies in Art and Poetry.* Finally, he gave the greatest attention to the print, paper, general makeup, even the advertisement of the book.[3]

After this edition of the *Renaissance* was issued, Pater apparently turned his main efforts to his new work. Just before the new edition appeared in April, 1877, he told Macmillan that he was working on the new volume of essays.[4] The table of contents he sent to Macmillan when he formally offered the book for publication (October 1, 1879) shows that only two of the essays had not been published previously. Two essays on Greek myth in two parts, an essay on Euripides, two essays on Shakespeare, an essay on Romanticism, one on Wordsworth, one on Lamb, and one on Venetian painting which was to be the title of the volume, "The School of Giorgione and other studies"—these were to be the diverse makeup of the book.[5] The book had none of the unity and coherence of the *Renaissance*, which may have caused misgivings to Pater, for his interests were here so farflung that titling was a question of simply deciding arbitrarily which essay would give the title to the book. This unhistorical quality is in clear contrast to most of Pater's literary projects. In the

Renaissance serious effort was made to show the flow and ebb
of intellectual and artistic influences within a fixed focus of
perception and response. Now Pater seemed to be satisfied to
follow this minute care with a divided collection with no special
integrating perspectives, no "original unity," as he later put it.
Perhaps this did bother him because he later retitled the collection, "Dionysus and Other Studies."[6] The essays were ready for
printing in November, 1878, and there seems to be a note of
urgency in Pater's letters to his publishers to get the book
through the press.[7] He was receiving proofs in later November,
and by the end of the month, he surprisingly changed his mind.
He wrote to Macmillan and asked that publication be halted
immediately; he offered to pay the costs of setting the type; he
supposed that the special paper that he had asked for could be
used for some other book; he called for his publisher's assent
forthwith. The reason was, he wrote, that the essays had "so
many inadequacies." Perhaps in the future they could be worked
into "a better and more complete form."[8] Macmillan tried to
persuade him to wait, but Pater had made up his mind. Pater
sent a check for thirty-five pounds to cover the cost of type-
setting on December 9 and asked that the type be broken up.[9]

There is no reason to doubt that Pater was genuinely dis-
satisfied with the quality of his work and thus cancelled its
publication. However, there is the additional possibility of
another, perhaps overriding, cause. There is good reason to suppose that public reception to his first publication gave Pater
serious doubts about his writing and, as has been suggested, this
caused him to seek some new mode of expression which would
carry his authentic self while providing a protective cover from
avid public scrutiny of his various states of mind and feeling
about his permanent interests. It seems that he was trying to
find the proper vehicle while carrying on the various literary
activities described above. As we shall see, he actually finished
one experiment which he saw fit to publish, he began another,
and the whole process was to become the creative base for a
magnum opus, a trilogy, the first of which was *Marius The
Epicurean*. The personal as well as creative implications behind

these efforts are very important in understanding Pater and his work.

Pater's literary ventures cannot be discussed apart from his cultural development. He told William Sharp as much when he described his literary work as "exclusively personal and solitary." Thus a brief accounting of the state of his permanent interests at the time of this important literary advance is pertinent. Fuller consideration in the larger context of his life, thought, and work will be made later.

The first phase of Pater's development, it will be remembered, was the shaping of a methodology of insight. How could he discover a focus through which he could see into the abiding causes of things? The first step was to count all the data of equal value at the outset. This meant clearing away all set perspectives and adjusted views. This is largely what he did in the early essays on Coleridge and Morris. In the former, he dismissed the traditional Christian attitudes with their absolutist metaphysics in favor of a humanism of complete culture. In the latter, he tried to put forth an evaluative regimen for his relativist spirit—the discipline and dedication of the empathic eye enriching the moment. Having now the procedure, Pater turned it on the art treasures of the fifteenth-century Italian Renaissance. The result was, of course, his study of the *Renaissance* with much of his Morris essay formulated into its "Conclusion."

Pater was not only professionally disconcerted over the reception of his book, as I have pointed out, but he experienced also deep spiritual unrest. This, of course, was most upsetting for a man given to solitary serenity and contemplative insight, as William Sharp depicted him. It seems that Pater particularly felt again the need for the kind of pure tranquillity he experienced at times as a child which his striving, austere, intense, and isolating philosophy in his *Renaissance* would not provide. How could he achieve some adult state which possessed the refinement of fully matured sensitivity within a life of abiding contentment?

Knowing that the peace of heart he once knew was ultimately a religious state, Pater began in 1878 attending the very Catholic liturgical services at St. Alban's, Holborn, and St. Austin's in the

New Kent Road. These highly ritualistic services, reviving the spirit of early Christianity, began to bring some rest to his disquietude and also rendered special satisfactions to his aesthetic nature. The return of a religious element into Pater's life seemed to give him a certain social solidarity, insofar as a solitary man senses society, while resisting the dangers of indiscriminate experience. He had rejected Christianity about ten years before, but now he found he needed it. Was religion somehow allied to beauty and hence art? His was a modern way of looking at things, a way that penetrated life and history—his own and the world's. Was a variety of religious experience possible for the modern mind?

Possessing the true philosophic instinct, he started with himself. The struggle was both literary and personal, though of course, for artists these categories are very likely logicalities. In any event, he had to probe his being—"that thick wall of personality," he called it—for traces of his true nature and then submit for evaluation his discovered person to those rational forces he deemed proper. This demanded what Pater himself called the services of philosophy, religion, and culture which had "to startle it [human nature] into sharp and eager observation." Pater was going through something like this when he decided to abandon his book of critical essays. Perhaps some breakthrough precipitated his decision.

Depth analysis is difficult, and Pater's was a painful case. The evidence for his struggles surfaces in his revealed literary plans, his failure to carry them out, and the state in which he abandoned them. The more one reads Pateriana, the more one is struck with both the literary and personal trials he suffered. There is not a reminiscence of this part of Pater's life that I know of which does not remark about a discernible quality of quiet sorrow he had, a heavy self-absorption which dislocated him from his surroundings.

Edmund Gosse wrote that Pater often relieved his tensions by resorting to childish fancy.[10] These mild regressions found their literary outlet in his venturing into the autobiographical essay. This was the first literary experiment on the way to *Marius*. Peter wrote "The Child in the House" and liked it enough to submit it to *Macmillan's Magazine* April 17, 1878.[11] He told the editor, George Grove, that it was not a part of a fictional work, but a complete work; he said that he hoped that this would be the first of a series which would have some sort of unity. He called the essay a portrait and explained that he meant the reader to experience the same intense interest in personality he might have on seeing a good portrait. Grove accepted the essay, and it was published in August, 1878. Pater still was not sure of himself. After he corrected the proof, he asked for another look at the revised version. He also asked that the article appear unsigned, but the editor apparently insisted, for it was signed.

It is fruitless to dispute how autobiographical "The Child in the House" is. Pater himself offered in his letter the key to its meaning, which was to reenact vividly and intensely the spirit of childhood through the medium of a literary portrait that by verbal power would strike the imagination as powerfully as a great portrait painting. The special touch he tried to achieve in "The Child in the House" was the growth of the delicate powers of a child's soul to that point of innocent loveliness where he begins to encounter a sense of loss, doom, and death—". . . the cry on the stair, sounding bitterly through the house, and struck into his soul forever. . . ." As Florian Deleal dreams of his childhood home, he knows that these tears foretell "the weariness of the way." It was of the same sights and sighs that Hopkins wrote in his lovely lyric "Spring and Fall."

When "The Child in the House" appeared, it was headed by the title *Imaginary Portraits,* and this sketch was numbered "I." Pater seems to have found a fresh way to interpret sympathetically his ruminations, for in September, 1878, Grove asked him to send the next installment. In December, Pater wrote him to tell him he would be unable to send the material because he was working on another sort of work. This work was very likely the second volume of essays. Scholars agree that this second installment was the unfinished "An English Poet," which was published posthumously.[12] Why did Pater stop his imaginary portraits? The likeliest conjecture, which is made by more than one student of Pater, is that the portraits were still too close to Pater's own life to be comfortable to him personally and to be readily acceptable to the Victorian public. He had to find a way to distance the subject so that the setting would better disguise those intimate elements which were so much a part of his work.

This was the genesis of *Marius*, I believe. By the end of 1878 Pater had stopped further work on his "imaginary portraits" and his new essay collection. He seemed to be clearing his desk for some long, careful preparation for writing a very large work. His publications during this time bear this out. Before 1879 he had averaged about one or two long essays a year, but between 1879 and 1885, the year of the publication of *Marius*, he published much less: three Greek studies and an essay on Rossetti. Given allowance for Pater's slow processes of writing, why did he devote so very much time to the making of *Marius*?

There is more than one reason. To speak of the literary first, Pater thought he had discovered in the "imaginary portrait" a secure way to handle his imaginative work. He said as much of "The Child in the House."[13] To this must be added that he found a way to distance his subject by the device of casting the portrait into an historical setting far from his own time, yet still being able to maintain personal and public currency through essential parallelisms—interpretative and evaluative—between his subject, the setting, and the modern mind. He chose Antonine Rome as meeting these requirements and set out to assimilate the historical material in preparation (including a trip to Rome in 1882) for his meticulous imaginative treatment.

Such prodigious efforts certainly promised an "imaginary portrait" larger than anything Pater had attempted previously. It was a test of imaginative powers to translate authentically the historical milieu into the portrait while giving the leading figure the dramatic revelation of a striking personality. Moreover, Pater, who considered himself a thinker and not just a stylist, as he told William Sharp, saw the possibility of imaginatively developing the intellectual aspect of his portrait, which is to say, have his figure represent some classic mode of thought. This provided a further opportunity. The rich historical period he had chosen was peopled with many possibilities of lesser portraits, background figures such as one finds in the crowd scenes in great portraits, which he had remarked about elsewhere. This afforded him the possibility of carrying on a kind of dialogue between the figures so that mental as well as moral implications would be reenacted. In shaping the portrait then, Pater was able to express his own evaluation of the thought, words, and actions and thus render a definitive projection of his subject. This quality is oven overlooked in *Marius*, despite the fact that Pater said in more than one place that such an evaluative element is a necessary requirement of all great art.

Of the personal reasons for taking so much time on *Marius*, more will be said later. It is enough to be reminded here that *Marius* represented for Pater a way to express his own need for religion and to provide a study for the degree of general applicability for his own time. This was perhaps one of his deepest personal problems, which he quite rightly tried to understand in the larger context of the intellectual crises of the nineteenth century. He wrote Violet Paget in July 1883, with *Marius* half-finished, about her article, "The Responsibilities of Unbelief: A Conversation Between Three Rationalists," telling her that there may very well be an other phase of the modern mind other than the epicure, the cultivated pessimist, and the humanitarian positivist. The other, he wrote, was a religious phase which is the very object of the design of *Marius*. The personal implications are intensified in his remarks to Miss Paget that he hoped to finish this large portrait soon since he wished to write many smaller ones which he preferred to do, yet he had to keep on with the big work because he felt it a "duty."[14] Putting this literary effort at this level of conscience certainly suggests Pater's deeply personal involvement in *Marius* and perhaps something of the obligations he felt to his time.

In June of 1884 Pater submitted *Marius* to *Macmillan's Magazine* to be published serially.[15] It was not accepted, so Pater offered it to Alexander Macmillan for general publication. *Marius* was issued March 4, 1885. Advance notice of the book was made in review by William Sharp, now Pater's good friend. Sharp in his personal reminiscences of Pater tells of getting proofs of *Marius* in advance of publication.[16]

By June, 1885, almost the entire first edition was sold out, and Pater eagerly planned with his publisher a second, less expensive edition.[17] This no doubt was greatly encouraging to him. Difficult as the writing of *Marius* was, he seriously considered more portraits on the same scale and order. He revealed his plans in a letter to an American journalist, Carl Wilhelm Ernst, in January, 1886.[18] He told Ernst that *Marius* was the first of a trilogy of similar works treating the same issues, but under different historical situations. The second was to take place in France at the end of the sixteenth century. The third, he thought, would be the end of the eighteenth century and the scene in England. Thus Pater's design shows that he wished to portray the Christian mind in different stages of its development. The second was to treat the spirit of medievalism trying to survive the Renaissance and encountering the Reformation; the third was to attempt to depict the Christian spirit confronting the age of Rationalism, science and the oncoming Romantic movement. Quite clearly, these projected books were of immense personal engagement as well as current philosophical magnitude.

It is sad and significant that Pater never completed his plan. However, he made a serious attempt. *Gaston De Latour* was to be part two of the trilogy. Thomas Wright said Pater began *Gaston* in June, 1888, but he was probably wrong about this since the first five chapters appeared serially in *Macmillan's Magazine* in 1888 from June through October. It is more likely that he was at work when he wrote of his plan to Carl Ernst in January, 1886. Charles Shadwell, who edited the unfinished *Gaston* after Pater's death, wrote in his preface that *Gaston* was probably begun shortly after *Marius* was completed. During this period Pater was not fully engaged with *Gaston* as he had been previously with *Marius*, for he worked on shorter portraits which, as he told Miss Paget, were "pleasanter" to him. Undoubtedly he had found a certain sense of execution, for he turned out seven of these short sketches between 1885 and 1893. All except two of them appeared in *Macmillan's Magazine*. Pater was also busy with preparing four of his portraits for publication as a volume for Macmillan with the title, *Imaginary Portraits*. This appeared in May, 1887. He told William Sharp that he considered including "The Child in the House," but that he felt he would have to make so many alterations, which he was disinclined to do, that he put it off for the time being.[19] Apparently Pater still felt the insufficiency of the disguise of his personal life in this portrait, and perhaps because he felt genuine endearment for the sketch in its original form, associating it, as I have noted previously, with the genesis of his new literary effort, he did not wish to touch it again. Arthur Symons gives the explanation that this first portrait was the first chapter of a romance, that it was full of autobiographical touches, and that since Pater always wanted to go on with it while half knowing that he never would, he did not reprint it.[20]

Benson called these portraits "a species of dreamy recitative." This describes the method of narration adequately, which is to say that quality of the telling of a mystery, but it does not attend to the one quality Pater strove for from the beginning—an image of a man heightened into a kind of total self-revelation, terrible to behold in all its vividness, but beguiling in all its strangeness. Moreover, in these later portraits Pater had achieved a way to handle objectively the personal stimulus to his work so that he quite confidently and successfully transposed his material into forms that were both interpretative and exemplary.

While *Gaston* languished, Pater went on to publications which were more in the line of "book business." A new edition of the *Renaissance* was brought out in 1888, in which he included his essay from his abandoned volume, "The School of Giorgione." Perhaps the most creative effort of this year, after *Gaston*, was his essay on "Style," which he published in the *Fortnightly Review*. The following year proved spare. Pater brought out a collection of assorted essays in a volume called *Appreciations with An Essay on Style*. All of its contents had been published previously. The book strikes one as the effort of a declining writer to get everything he wishes on record.

It is true that Pater was still trying to do imaginative work. He did another short portrait, "Hippolytus Veiled." He was even trying to go on with *Gaston*. In August, 1889, he published what was to be the substance of Chapter 7 of *Gaston*, "Giordano Bruno." But more and more, he found himself doing something else. Interspersed with the short portraits already mentioned, he wrote some reviews, delivered some lectures, and gradually turned his attention to one of his lifelong interests—Plato and Greece. These writings began to appear in 1892. It seems that Pater decided to have one more effort at showing that he deserved his Oxford Fellowship, that he possessed those energies of mind necessary for what in his day was called "an Oxford scholar." His *Plato and Platonism* (1893) did change some minds, Jowett's for one.

Arthur Symons noted that in 1889, Pater was planning another volume of "Imaginary Portraits."[21] He refers to those portraits that Pater subsequently wrote as intended for this book along with some that were never written. He wrote that Pater planned to follow his *Appreciations* with a volume of Greek studies, that he had thought of putting together a book of "theory," which would include the essay on "Style." Of more interest to us here, he hoped to finish *Gaston* in two or three years. He was at work on it in 1890, even hoped to try to finish it during the summer of that year.[22] At some time during this period, Pater gave up his trilogy, the grandest literary scheme he ever envisioned, the most demanding of his literary powers, a plan that would perhaps have been one of the most important artistic and intellectual works of his era.

Of his many changes of mind and abandoned projects, none is more important than his quitting *Gaston*, yet very little is known about Pater's reasons for this. Wright thought it was stopped because Pater became unhappy with the story structure.[23] Charles Shadwell tells us nothing of Pater's actions in his edition of *Gaston* except that for posterity he underlined Pater's broken hopes by adding the subtitle, *An Unfinished Romance*. From the unfinished fragments among Pater's papers, Shadwell inserted what Pater intended as a sixth chapter (which Pater called "Shadows of Events") in order to fill the gap in what had already been published, the first five chapters and Chapter 7. Pater had actually worked on chapters 8 to 13; he may indeed have compiled a few notes toward the third book,[24] but Shadwell explained in his preface that ". . . nothing more remains in his writings in a shape sufficiently finished for publication. . . ."[25]

A. C. Benson generally followed Wright's explanation: "I am

myself disposed to think that he found the historical setting too complicated and the canvas too much crowded." Benson wrote that Gaston loses individuality, as the story progresses, that he becomes little more than a focus for a myriad of events, that the issues get so complicated that Pater knew himself to be failing to cope with the literary situation.[26] Surprisingly, among those friends and acquaintances who have written of Pater—Sharp, Gosse, Paget, Symons, Johnson, Wilde—none ventures an explanation. They very probably did not have one, for if Pater was reserved about most of his person, there is little doubt that the slow death of his grand scheme went on unobtrusively behind that high wall of his impervious personality.

Therefore, we are left to speculate why Pater stopped his work in which he had already invested a great deal of time and energy and had publicly committed his literary reputation by allowing a large portion to be published, and why he continued to tell his friends that he hoped to complete the book. To those speculations already mentioned, a few can be added. One is that Pater was overburdened with activities. Some of Pater's time was taken helping Arthur Symons prepare a book of verse, which Pater agreed to do in January, 1888. In the same year he began suffering from gout which at times confined him to his rooms. Pater was very generous in helping Symons, as Symons later recalled, even though the effort lasted over a year. When the book appeared early in 1889, Pater wrote a kind review in the *Pall Mall Gazette*.[27]

Pater spend a good deal of time and effort presiding over his literary reputation which by then was large. Notable people wanted to meet him; literary personages were reviewing his newest publications, reviews which often required acknowledgment.[28] Pater was asked to lecture. He was asked to hear lectures.[29] Writers sent him presentation copies of their work for his acceptance and approval, and Pater was not one to be ungracious. He tried to read them and write the authors of his impressions.[30] He was asked to sit for a portrait by William Rothenstein. He agreed to do so, but he disliked the drawing (as did his sisters) and stoutly opposed its publication.[31] He was asked to contribute to new magazines. Arthur Symons asked for something for the *Yellow Book*, but Pater was too busy.[32] Pater was even given an honorary degree of LL.D., for which occasion he traveled to Glasgow to have it conferred on April 13, 1894.[33]

Remembering that Pater was carrying on his academic work at Oxford (not as a tutor after 1884), that he was pursuing his critical studies of Greece along with some efforts on his imaginative writing, that he was as usual steering his books through the publication process with the greatest care, that he was still trying to do some traveling both for pleasure as well as aesthetic profit—it is not farfetched to suggest that Pater did not have the time or energy to properly work on *Gaston*. This is certainly true if the composition of *Marius* is taken as the norm of required engagement to complete such an undertaking. On the other hand, a writer gives to each individual work what it demands in proportion to his creative spur. Herein lies the riddle of Pater's failure.

I believe all of the aforementioned conjectures are only contributory to the real reason for Pater's inability to carry off his major literary plans. The true reason lies in his religious dilemma. Edmund Gosse was closer to the truth when he wrote, "He was not all for Apollo, nor all for Christ, but each deity swayed in him, and neither had that perfect homage that brings peace behind it." Pater's trilogy was to be the gospel of the pilgrimage of men's souls to come to spiritual perfection, the union of all goodness and beauty and truth. All wayfarers have come to know "the weariness of the way," but Pater experienced that extra burden of not being able to sacrifice easily his myriad sympathies to the strait way of the Lord.

II

Hopkins' "counterpoise"

In an exchange of letters during November and December, 1881, R. W. Dixon and G. M. Hopkins discussed poetry and the priesthood. Dixon said, "Surely one vocation cannot destroy another: and such a Society as yours will not remain ignorant that you have such gifts as have seldom been given by God to man."[34] Hopkins responded with a long explanation of his notion of "God's service" and his views on the Jesuits and culture. Pointing out that the Society had sometimes contributed to culture in its service to God, he noted ". . . that literature proper, as poetry, has seldom been found to be to that end a very serviceable means . . . there have been very few Jesuit poets and, where they have been, I believe it would be found on examination that there was something exceptional in their circumstances or, so to say, counterbalancing in their career."[35] Here Hopkins launched into a survey of Jesuits who attained distinction of one sort or another. In each instance, he pointed out counterbalancing religious elements in their lives which neutralized the dangers of individual fame: "In England we had Fr. Southwell, a poet, a minor poet but still a poet; but he wrote amidst a terrible persecution and died a martyr, with circumstances of horrible barbarity: this is the counterpoise in his career."[36]

While there is no rancor in his letter, more a quelling of Dixon's astonishment, the explanation offered describes the precarious predicament of Hopkins' poetic genius. What he really was telling the Anglican canon was that he had as yet no "counterpoise" in his career which would give him justification to write less spasmodically or even publish occasionally. I do not mean to suggest that Hopkins was looking for an excuse. What he did want very much was to make something of his priesthood, both professionally and spiritually. A good and God-fearing man, Dixon was amazed and saddened that Hopkins seemed to think that his poetry was very much of an aside to his praising and serving God. And so has been almost everyone since. Nevertheless, Hopkins believed what he wrote. How he lived it is his story, the search for a "counterpoise" for his muse.

III

A priest-poet needed a "counterpoise." Hopkins dimly perceived this when he decided to take holy orders: "I want to write still and as a priest I very likely can do that too, not so freely as I should have liked, e.g. nothing or little in the verse way, but no doubt what would best serve the cause of my

religion."[37] He calmly affirmed harmony between his two voca-
tions. To be sure, the priesthood was to take the lead, but he
hoped that the "Jesuit Discipline"[38] would not be too hard on
the poet. He probably burned his poetry with some equanimity
when he entered the Jesuit order, though he called it a
"slaughter."

Even in 1875, there was no cause for anxiety over poetry. His
superior had expressed the wish for a poem on the *Deutschland*
wreck,[39] and Hopkins responded with a long, ornate ode full of
the sound and fury of stormy salvation.[40] With his ordination in
1877, the prospects of a more substantial "counterpoise" than
the hint of a superior was in the offing. While the missions were
not likely, the pursuit of advanced theology was possible.

While at Oxford, Hopkins had shown enough interest in
philosophy to formulate a theory of ideogenesis as his essays on
words and Parmenides show.[41] Already in 1868 he had begun
developing his notion of "inscape," "stressing," and "instress."
So it was quite natural that when he began his philosophy as a
Jesuit, he picked up where he left off. But in doing the first
course, psychology, he received little inspiration, for he was
taught the rational psychology of Francisco Suarez (a sixteenth-
century Jesuit theologian who attempted to amalgamate the
various Scholastic trends into one main system) who emphasized
the Aristotelian-Aquinian epistemological tradition rather than
the Platonic-Augustinian. Put over-simply, this meant that Hopkins was taught that all human knowledge is obtained only
through abstracting the senses, thus eliminating the theory of
intuitive knowledge.

Hopkins was disenchanted when he finished his course in
1872.[42] Suarez was of no avail to his speculations. Surely, in the
Scholastic tradition, there must be one whose perspectives would
be more accommodating to his own theories, while still being
a rather complete, equally compelling, fully orthodox thinker.
His *Journal* records for August 3, 1872: "At this time I had first
begun to get hold of the copy of Scotus on the Sentences in the
Baddely library and was flush with a new stroke of enthusiasm.
It may come to nothing or it may be a mercy from God. But just

then when I took in any inscape of the sky or sea I thought of Scotus."[43]

It came to nothing as the "counterpoise" he was seeking. Hopkinsians will not like this, and they will point to interesting aesthetic and theological speculation which Scotus occasioned in Hopkins.[44] I am of no mind to deny a certain brilliance to Hopkins' theological speculation nor an engaging sketch of a theory of aesthetics. Even the little of both he left in his writings indicates the originality and range of his mind. Still, after his ordination, his Jesuit preceptors denied him the further year of theological studies which would have set him on a path to a professorship in theology or scripture. He might have had his "counterpoise." He seemed to offer considerable promise. The historian of University College, Dublin, remembered the promise and the difficulty: ". . . as a theologian his undoubted brilliance was dimmed by a somewhat obstinate love of Scotist doctrine, in which he traced the influence of Platonist philosophy. His idiosyncrasy got him into difficulty with his Jesuit preceptors. . . ."[45]

IV

Preaching the word of God is one of the prime duties of holy orders. It would most certainly qualify as a licit means of employing talent. Hopkins began his career at the famous London church known as "Farm Street" with a series of three sermons in August of 1878. As his letters to Bridges indicate, he was most confident and eager. In November he was moved to Oxford to serve the parish church of St. Aloysius. The move seemed helpful, for there was the possibility that he might have become a sort of chaplain to the Catholics at the university, a post where his talents and experience could have been beneficial.

Within a year, Hopkins was dispatched again. His year at Oxford was a disappointment. He seemed indisposed to serve either the Town or the Gown. He did not have a thriving relationship with his superior, Father T. B. Parkinson, who kept university relationships in his own hands. At a suggestion of a colleague, Fr. William Humphrey, Hopkins began writing out his sermons. We have six from his last three months at Oxford. While some are brilliant with rhetorical effect, they lack what Hopkins himself was to call *bidding,* "the art or virtue of saying everything right *to* or *at* the hearer, interesting him, holding him."[46]

His next assignment was a big parish church in Liverpool, St. Francis Xavier's. But before taking up residence in Liverpool he was to put in three months at Bedford Leigh, a small industrial town near Manchester. Here he seems to have found himself as a preacher, perhaps, because he felt for the first time the shepherdry of the priesthood. Whatever his satisfaction was, his letters and sermons ebb and flow in the full tide of "bidding." He told his friend Baillie: "Oxford was not to me a congenial field, fond as I am of it; I am more at home with the Lancashire people."[47]

The Bedford Leigh sermons are filled with homey words of simple piety. They were a modest success, and more than likely Hopkins went on to Liverpool with something of a preaching reputation. At least when he arrived he was immediately assigned to give a course of four Sunday evening sermons in a pulpit regularly occupied by distinguished preachers who spoke to very large crowds. Here was a first-rate opportunity to establish a reputation.

He began satisfactorily with a sermon on the theme, "Duty is Love." Its directness and simplicity were promising. In the second of the series he launched into the first of a trilogy on "The Kingdom of God." Hopkins had some original notions on this subject, aided and abetted by Scotus (whom he had been reading since 1872). He announced his plan: ". . . tonight therefore let our thoughts be turned to God's kingdom as it was first founded upon earth and next Sunday we shall, I hope, see its history, its glory, and its fall."[48]

In order to put across this recondite theological subject, Hopkins resorted to political idiom: "God is our king." He skillfully drew his version of the compact of *original justice* (immunity from sin and concupiscence); he ended by announcing: "And all fell, all is gone. . . ."[49] Now, with the grandiosity of this matter, his full powers were being called into action, not only his expressive ability, but also his creativity. His superior may have discerned that his parish was in for some original theological speculation, and the new man did not allay these feelings in his next sermon.

A week later Hopkins examined in detail the terms of God's compact with man and the consequences of its breaching. He overran his time, and again he ended on the note of the dissolution of God's kingdom. Whether the rector of the parish, Father James Clare, understood the original blend of Aquinas and Scotus that Hopkins was expressing, I do not know. A fine preacher himself, he may very well have become disturbed with the young priests' sense of dialectic. Twice Hopkins had ended on very negative notes, and then he entitled his next effort, "On the Fall of God's First Kingdom." It was too much, as the note Hopkins wrote over the text sadly records: "I was not allowed to take this title and on the printed bills it was covered by a blank slip pasted over. The text too I changed to last week's, and had to leave out or reword all passages speaking of God's kingdom as falling."[50] This undoubtedly hurt the young curate, for two years later he returned to this climactic sermon and wrote a long explanatory note. It suggests his curtailment was something more than bad preaching strategy.

For three months he was not called on to preach. Then he was named again to preach the Sunday gospel of April 25, but a note appended to the sermon indicates discouragement: "Notes (for it seems that written sermons do no good)."[51] The sermon is a brilliant example of his exegetical ability. He was called on again for Sunday, May 30. Again he wrote a fine exegesis of the parable of the supper and the guests who would not come, but it was not given. A visitor took his place. This happened again on June 29, 1880. He remained fifteen months more at Liverpool and was asked to preach only three more Sunday sermons.[52] One of these is a great sermon, a combination of spiritual insight and verbal eloquence which was beyond the capacities of his listeners.

But the disappointments were welling up. He preached on short notice one of his sermons from Bedford Leigh.[53] At first he was pleased, for he seemed to have moved some of his hearers to tears, but when he preached a week later, he noted drearily, ". . . but when the thing happened next week I perceived that it was hot and that it was sweat they were wiping away."[54] Whether they were or not, there is little question about Hopkins. On October 25, 1880, he preached on "Divine Providence and the Guardian Angels." The fourth line of the sermon reads, "He [God] takes more interest in a merchant's business than the merchant, in a vessel's steering than the pilot, in a lover's sweetheart than the lover, in a sick man's pain than the sufferer, in our salvation than we ourselves." The line is broken with a crushing note: "[In consequence of this word *sweetheart* I was in a manner suspended and at all events was forbidden (it was some time after) to preach without having my sermon revised. However, when I was going to take the next sermon I had to give after this regulation came into force to Fr. Clare for revision he poohpoohed the matter and would not look at it.]"[55] There are three more extant sermons, and Hopkins states he preached more that he did not write down. However, the record of his disillusion is clear.

When he was assigned to Liverpool, Hopkins surmised he was in for a trying time. His letters document the unfortunate fulfillment. His first letter to Dixon from Liverpool answers the canon's request for more of Hopkins' poetry: "The parish work of Liverpool is very wearing to mind and body and leaves me nothing but odds and ends of time."[56] This was May 14. Two weeks before he had told his mother of his illness during the Easter season when work was the heaviest: "Neither am I very strong now and as long as I am in Liverpool I do not see how I can be; not that I complain of this, but I state it."[57] He told his friend Baillie, on May 22: "At least I can say my Liverpool work is very harassing and makes it hard to write."[58]

By September he was caving in both physically and spiritually. He opened his letter to Bridges on September 5: "I take up a languid pen to write you, being down with diarrhoea and vomiting, brought on by yesterday's heat and the long hours in the confessional."[59] Again in October: "I daresay you have long expected . . . an answer. . . . But I never could write; time and spirits were wanting; one is so fagged, so harried and gallied up and down. And the drunkards go on drinking, the filthy, as the scripture says, are filthy still: human nature is so inveterate. Would that I had seen the last of it."[60] And he still had almost a full year to go! But he wearied his way through.

Hopkins was assigned on October 10, 1881, to begin his third year of noviceship (tertianship) before taking his final vows. He was to go back where he had begun it all, Manresa House, Roehampton, and he welcomed the change and the chance to survey the damage: ". . . I feel that I need the noviceship very much and shall be every way better off when I have been made more spiritual minded."[61] As we shall see, he did recoup enough to begin all over.

As for his preaching, it would be unfair to say that Hopkins was decidedly a failure. Reading his sermons, one is often struck by their fresh theological perspectives, the courage to attack difficult sermon topics, and a frequent brilliance and beauty of composition. As for the spiritual value afforded to those who heard them, we shall never know. His short stature and high-pitched voice certainly were handicaps when coupled with his chronic inability to estimate his congregations—and his superiors! Professionally speaking though, Father Clare's "pooh-poohing" is the keynote to the preaching "counterpoise" in G. M. Hopkins.

V

The year of tertianship (1881-82) proved, as Hopkins had hoped it would, to be a period of regeneration. He began it very hopefully. After explaining to Dixon that tertianship is a second noviceship in preparation for taking last vows and asserting his fidelity to his vocation, he commented: "Besides all which, my mind is here more at peace than it has ever been and I would gladly live all my life, if it were so to be, in as great or a greater seclusion from the world and be busied only with God."[62] His first letter to Bridges from Roehampton is filled with new fervor and buoyancy: "This spot, though it has suffered much from decay of nature and more from the hand of man, is still beautiful. It is besides a great rest to be here and I am in a very contented frame of mind."[63]

It proved to be a wonderfully creative year. Hopkins wrote the bulk of his spiritual writing during this year (nearly one hundred printed pages) and laid down plans for five different works: a commentary on the *Spiritual Exercises* (which he began during a month's meditation on them), a study of sacrifice in ancient religions, a treatise on the lyric art of Greece, an ode on Edmund Campion, and a drama based on the life of St. Winefred. So he had projected three works in prose and two in verse. If not as a theologian or a preacher, then he might find his counterbalance as a scholar (sometimes writer)—an endeavor highly suitable to his talents.

It is not relevant here to examine the many insights and comments he made on the *Spiritual Exercises* during his second noviceship.[64] However, there are two aspects of his spiritual writings which bear on Hopkins' "counterpoise." One is his ever-deepening conviction of the kind of "counterpoise" that there must be in his life. His inspiration here was the life of Christ. He called it "the great sacrifice" of Christ. It was based on St. Paul's Epistle to the Philippians (ii, 5-11). In sum it was that Christ performed three great acts of sacrifice by making Himself subservient to His Father, to the angels and to men: ". . . he emptied or exhausted himself so far as that was possible, of godhead and behaved only as God's slave, as his creature, as man, which he also was, and then being in the guise of man humbled himself to death, the death of the cross." He had a light on how the incarnation shaped the lives of men: "It is this holding of himself back, and not snatching at the truest and highest good, the good that was his right, nay his possession from a past eternity in his other nature, his own being and self, which seems to me the root of all his holiness and the imitation of this the root of all moral good in men."[65] The "counterpoise" must be determined by Christ.

The other note is equally important. It might be called "personality and the counterpoise." Victorianism itself called for a kind of counterbalance in life, and I offer the opinion that the greatest evidence of this lies in the religious sensibility of that day which asserted an inevitable strife between personality and goodness. I think that this is nowhere more evident in the life of a Victorian than it is in the life of Hopkins. One would have expected Hopkins to have been duly influenced as a Jesuit by the great emphasis St. Ignatius puts upon the notion that true charity lies in the union of duty and desire, or integrated personality. The whole design of the *Spiritual Exercises* is to achieve this end. St. Ignatius' famous letters on obedience offer counsels on obtaining this state within the Society of Jesus.

Moreover, Scotus, Hopkins' "rarest-veined unraveller," stressed, contrary to the Victorian code, that desire and choice should go together. If there is inevitable opposition between the two, human personality is traumatically bifurcated, and man's psychic state is thus perpetually anxious, and in a state of deep, internal conflict. But this is not normal personality, and all of Hopkins' spiritual guides told him so.

Though there is good reason to believe that Hopkins knew this, still, in his writings on human personality, he says that human nature and personality are arbitrarily joined.[66] So it follows that there can be no natural impulse to goodness or God, for all impetus must come from an act of choice or through the "elective will." Duty, then, is a struggle against our nature to do that which is either repugnant or indifferent to our "affective" selves. Why Hopkins should have continued to exaggerate the distinction between our "elective" and "affective" selves, I do not know, but it does amount to a kind of adjustment of the Ignatian view of personality to that of Victorian Protestantism. As we shall see, this view of personality coupled with the "great sacrifice" was in the time of crisis to show the way to spiritual heroism and tragedy.

VI

After Hopkins made his Last Vows, he was appointed to teach classics at Stonyhurst: "My appointment is to teach our 'philosophers' (like undergraduate students) Latin, Greek, and perhaps hereafter English (when I know more about it) for the

London B.A. degree."[67] The time certainly seemed propitious for some serious writing, for Hopkins was now in happy circumstances as his letters show. The only question was the approval of his Provincial (the superior for all English Jesuits). Accordingly, Hopkins outlined some of his interests to his superior, and while he did not receive strong encouragement, he was not prohibited. He reported his interview to Bridges: "The Provincial further added that what time was left over I might employ in writing one or other of the books I had named to him. But very little time will be left over and I cd. never make time."[68] But could he get anything done if there were time? He closed the paragraph quoted above with a worry: "Indeed now, with nothing to do but prepare, I cannot get forward with my ode. But one must hope against hope."

There was, in fact, time and Hopkins was making some use of it. By early October he had finished the choruses for *St. Winefred's Well.* Apparently he had Beuno's speech by December. Yet something was wrong. He told his dear friend Baillie: "I am here to coach classics. . . . I like my pupils and do not wholly dislike the work, but I fall into or continue in a weary state of body and mind . . . I make no way with what I read, and seem but half a man."[69] He told Bridges in March the same, and by June Dixon had heard.

The listlessness and ennui continued until the autumn of 1883. Even his meeting with Coventry Patmore on July 29, 1883 (when Patmore was on a visit to Stonyhurst) did not spark Hopkins. It is true that they struck off a warm friendship: they exchanged letters, and Hopkins assisted Patmore with a new edition of his *Poems* by offering a considerable number of suggestions and evaluations. Hopkins visited briefly with Patmore at his home in Hastings during August 1885. Whatever impetus there might have been, it fell far short, perhaps because of what had transpired when he made his retreat at Beaumont in September of 1883.

Hopkins jotted down a page and a half of private notes[70] he made during his retreat, but their brevity, in my opinion, belies their importance. First, in meditating on his sins, he became so upset that he was advised (a suggestion that was frequent) to leave off considering them. While there is some question whether Hopkins was scrupulous, there is no question that his conscience was a hard taskmaster. Second, he considered his religious performance cowardly and had to settle for trying to perform well his ordinary duties. Third, "During this retreat I have much and earnestly prayed that God will lift me above myself to a higher state of grace, in which I may have more union with him, be more zealous to do his will, and freer from sin."

But how was this to be? He had failed to make any significant contribution to the Society either as a theologian or preacher. It now seemed that nothing was to come of his professional writing. As he himself said, ". . . I do little in the way of hard penances. . . ." He could perform his ordinary duties well, for he had been assured this was a "great part of life" of the holiest men. Surely though, there was something more he could do, some little sacrifice not unworthy the "great sacrifice." Was there a "counterpoise" for him?

There was only one thing he could do: "Also in some med. today I earnestly asked our Lord to watch over my compositions, not to preserve them from being lost or coming to nothing, for that I am very willing they should be, but they might not do me harm through enmity or imprudence of any man or my own; that he should have them as his own and employ or not employ them as he should see fit. And this I believe is heard." This offering, viewed in the light of Hopkins' own psychology and Ignatian spirituality, must be taken to mean that he had chosen to detach himself from his poetry to the point of personal indifference. The poems were to be no longer a real concern. In effect, what Hopkins was doing was bringing his desires into line with his choice of closer union with God. It did not mean that he would write no more; it meant that what he had written or would write was left to its own destiny.

But can one give up one's special self like this? The next day after Hopkins had had his "great grace," he had another insight: "In meditating on the Crucifixion I saw how my asking to be raised to a higher degree of grace was asking also to be lifted higher on the cross." And the next day: "The walk to

Emmaus. This morning in Thanksgiving after mass much bitter thought but also insight in things. And the above meditation was made in a desolate frame of mind; but towards the end I was able to rejoice in the comfort our Lord gave those two men. . . ." More desolation and the loss of comfort would bring him down to cases where ". . . thoughts against/thoughts in groans grind." There would be no carols in his "counterpoise."

VII

The last years of Hopkins' life are such a wrestling for salvation that they are almost a morality play in five acts. They begin with his "exile" to Ireland in 1884: "To seem the stranger lies my lot, my life/Among strangers."[71] His first letter to Bridges from Dublin sets the stage: "I have been warmly welcomed and most kindly treated. But Dublin itself is a joyless place and I think in my heart as smoky as London is: I had fancied it quite different."[72] Six weeks later in a letter to Baillie,[73] physical and mental deterioration was setting in: "The melancholy I have all my life been subject to has become of late years not indeed more intense in its fits but rather more distributed, constant and crippling. One, the lightest but a very inconvenient form of it, is daily anxiety about work to be done, which makes me break off or never finish all that lies outside that work. It is useless to write more on this: when I am at my worst, though my judgment is never affected, my state is much like madness." The closing lines foreshadow the tragic end of the conflict: "I see no ground for thinking I shall ever get over it or succeed in doing anything that is not forced on me to do of any consequence." Thus went the prologue.

The first act (1885) is full of passion and poetry: "To what serves Mortal Beauty?" ". . . Our evening is over us; our night whelms, whelms/and will end us." "But ah, but O thou terrible, why wouldst thou rude on me/Thy wring-world right foot rock?" "Comforter, where, where is your comforting?" "And my lament/Is cries countless, cries like dead letters sent/To dearest him that lives alas! away." "We hear our hearts grate on themselves: it kills/To bruise them dearer." "I cast for comfort I can no more get. . . ."[74]

The next three acts (1886-88) are filled with prosaic attrition. They are gradual in movement, their very pace illustrative of the passing of vitality. Despite moments of critical acumen and periods of calm, quite ugly shapes of slavery and madness lurk in Hopkins' letters of this period—even suicide. He was being destroyed by his "counterpoise" but believing this all he had to offer, he desperately clung to his choice. There is even some sign of his dissatisfaction with God's justice in the face of his difficult decision. It apparently never occurred to him that what he was attempting was as unnatural as a father being indifferent to the fate of his children. Though the destruction of the spirit is often latent, its effects silent beneath the surface, there comes that sudden moment when the harsh, grating voice of ravage speaks: "All impulse fails me: I can give myself no sufficient reason for going on. Nothing comes: I am a eunuch—but it is for the kingdom of heaven's sake."[75]

Conventionally, the last act of a morality play is the soul's reckoning. Hopkins' last retreat (January, 1889) before his death serves the convention well. The place is St. Stanislaus' College, Tullabeg, Ireland. This was the novitiate of the Irish Province of Jesuits. His retreat notes[76] (four double sheets of notepaper closely written on both sides) provide the drama.

The first three days are a ruthless self-examination of his life: "The question is how I advance the side I serve on." He considers his public service in Ireland, the distressing state of Irish politics, and the questionable patriotism of the Irish Church. The accusation is strong: "I do not feel then that outwardly I do much good, much that I care to do or can much wish to prosper; and this is a mournful life to lead."

But did his inner disposition acquit him? The consideration was wracking: "I was continuing this train of thought this evening when I began to enter on that course of loathing and helplessness which I have so often felt before, which made me feel madness. . . . I could therefore do no more than repeat *Justus es, Domine, et rectum judicium tuum* and the like. . . .

What is my wretched life? Five wasted years almost have passed
in Ireland. I am ashamed of the little I have done, of my waste
of time, although helplessness and weakness is such that I could
scarcely do otherwise. And yet the Wise Man warns us against
excusing ourselves in that fashion. I cannot then be excused;
but what is life without aim, without spur, without help? All
my undertakings miscarry: I am like a straining eunuch. I wish
then for death: yet if I died now I should die imperfect, no
master of myself, and that is the worst failure of all. O my God,
look down on me."

The second day: "This morning I made the meditation on
the Three Sins, with nothing to enter but loathing of my life
and a barren submission to God's will." The third day: "Help-
less loathing." The fourth day there are no notes. On the fifth
day, he reconsidered the Incarnation: "The Incarnation was
for my salvation and that of the world: the work goes on in
a great system and machinery which even drags me on with
the collar round my neck though I could and do neglect my
duty in it. But I say to myself that I am only too willing to do
God's work and help on the knowledge of the Incarnation. But
this is not really true: I am not willing enough for the piece of
work assigned me, the only work I am given to do, though I
could do others if they were given."

But he had done something leading from the Incarnation:
"And I thought that the Royal University was to me what
Augustus's enrollment was to St. Joseph: *exiit sermo a Caesare
Augusto etc.*; so the resolution of the R.U. came to me, incon-
venient and painful, but the journey to Bethlehem was incon-
venient and painful; and then I am bound in justice, and paid."
He had some spiritual footing upon which to find equilibrium,
and he strained for his balance: "I hope to bear this in mind."

Relief came the same day though he did not write it down
until the next: "Yesterday I had ever so much light . . . and
last night . . . and today . . . more than I can easily put down."
The light is on the Epiphany. His editor, Father Christopher
Devlin, described the entries: "In these last notes all is juice
sucked from the words of the gospel, nothing is spun from
fancy." Fr. Devlin also provided a comment on the moral drama:

"They end with the cliff-face scaled and his mind at one, striding forward with great strides on a high plateau of light; of light, or rather of bright shadow. . . ."[77]

I think "bright shadow" is the way the drama ends. It is true that in his last letters, Hopkins, is often in good spirits despite a continual deterioration of his health. Indeed, at the onset of his final sickness, a month before he died, he wrote to his mother: "My sickness falling at the most pressing time of the University work, there will be the devil to pay. Only there is no harm in saying, that gives *me* no trouble but an unlooked for relief. At many such a time I have been in a sort of extremity of mind, now I am the placidest soul in the world. And you will see, when I come round, I shall be the better for this."[78]

But then the darkness was never done. There is the appeal in his sonnet of March: "Mine, O thou lord of life, send my roots rain." Even more significant is the last poem he sent to Bridges in April. Though it is entitled, "To R.B.," it is really an epitaph to his muse: "My winter world, that scarcely breathes. . . ." Twenty-one years before, Hopkins burnt his verse ". . . as not belonging to my profession. . . ."[79] He did not realize, in his religious exuberance, that he had set himself on fire. Perhaps he had his "counterpoise" from that moment on. When he recognized it finally, he too ". . . found it an intolerable grief to submit to it,"[80] but there is also a splendor in his submission. It is the dark light of tragedy.

CHAPTER IV

Temper and Inscape

I

TIME MAKES A CARICATURE of truth. And so in their judgments of Hopkins and Pater, scholars have not avoided making cartoons. Pater is pictured as a supersensitive impressionist, sick with a high aesthetic temperature; Hopkins is shown as a haloed Jesuit, pale from an acute temptation for poetry. As in all good cartoons, there is some truth in these impressions; the danger is that in their pastoral simplicity they might be taken as true portraits.

In an attempt to obtain a truer likeness, I should like to suggest some different perspectives. It is not so much a question of erasing lines already drawn, but rather an effort to add more and different planes and colors to the design in hope that the picture will be richer and truer. I should like to draw in the following: Hopkins was an ardent Romantic wearing a tight clerical collar; Pater was a traditional humanist having a snit with orthodoxy. Let us begin with Hopkins.

The Romantic spirit was essentially a mentality about the true meaning of human experience. This mentality had three sides. The first was that in our senses we truly encounter the reality of existence and thus this knowledge is primal to all human knowledge. The second was that through sense knowledge the mind sees intuitively and comprehensively the concrete uniqueness of the presences in Nature. The third was that such comprehensive intuitive awareness discerned a summary presence in and behind Nature in the encounter of which, a bond is established that is sacred and sublime. These three attributes are in the English Romantics, especially the first generation, but they form the core of Romanticism wherever its spirit thrived. A re-reading of Wordsworth's "Tintern Abbey" reveals them clearly and distinctly. Hopkins himself recognized this in Wordsworth and honored it in his judgment of the great Romantic:

What I suppose grows on people is that Wordsworth's particular grace, his *charisma,* as theologians say, has been granted in equal measure to so very few men since times was [sic]—to Plato and who else? I mean his spiritual insight into nature; and this they perhaps think is above all the poet's gift? It is true, if we sort things, so that art is art and philosophy philosophy, it seems rather the philosopher's than the poet's: at any rate he had it in a sovereign degree. He had a "divine philosophy" and a lovely gift of verse. . . .

It is the Romantic *charisma* I wish to underline and its tradition I wish to suggest.

Now the Romanticism I have distilled here did not, unfortunately, exist in its pure state anywhere in the nineteenth century, though I believe it was purer in Wordsworth and Coleridge than on the Continent. By pure I mean a Romanticism which was a continuation of the Humanism which had burst forth again in the Renaissance—a new appreciation of the nature of man, his goodness and his dignity which rested on a natural theology for its rational optimism. Of course, the Humanism of the sixteenth century was not the Humanism of the eighteenth, which was what the Romantics inherited, for by this time a number of corruptions had set in. Descartes had driven the first knife into natural theology by divorcing matter and spirit, thus undercutting the very ground of Humanism: the world was a rational order which could only be explained as the work of divine Reason. The second corruption came from the new scientific learning. The new scientists argued that their studies were even greater confirmation of the rational order of the universe, and thus they depended heavily upon the idea of God as the source and principle of order. But while superficially they seemed to strengthen the natural theology of Humanism, in fact they dealt it a serious blow, for they not only affimed God as the author of Nature, they also made Him the very medium and guarantee of their knowledge. Thus God became a mathematical idea which Christians like Pascal cried out against. Humanism was not, of course, decomposed immediately by these debilitating forces. As long as it could maintain some contact with the tradition of Christian culture still existing, it remained vital. But when these disordering forces came to a focal point of intensity, as they did in name of Deism, the vital connection was broken. Natural theology became a purely rational religion unable to withstand the attacks of the skeptics. Moreover, Deists did little countering because Deism was never a religion in the first place. It was just the empiricists' Sunday amusement. Humanism had lost its principle of order.

Students of the Enlightenment will be quick to point out that Natural Theology survived the eighteenth century, which of course it did, but in a rather dry, apologetical, and impoverished way. This is another way of saying Humanism was floundering in seeking a mode of intelligibility. And so naturally it began to be taken up into the eddying currents of what was a changing culture. Among these were the emotionalism of Rousseau and the spiritualism of Oriental religion. What was really happening to Humanism was that it was slowly being permeated by science until there emerged in the nineteenth century a Humanism which was irreligious and unspiritual, a Rationalist Humanism to go along with a secular culture.

I believe the English Romanticists in general, Wordsworth and Coleridge especially, were basically Humanists who still had a very deep sense of traditional Humanism with its natural theological fundament. And while it is true that both Wordsworth and Coleridge were influenced by the sediment of Deism, the philosophy of the empiricists, the idealists, and the emotionalists, they clung to the awareness of the supreme value of Nature and Man in the sustaining presence of God. Moreover, they were acutely aware of the threats to this holy bond which were coming from all sides, and so their Humanism was in a kind of constant vacillation as they tried to find a natural theology on which to ground their lives and their art. It is no small surprise that they often sound merely subjectivist or eclectic, for they really had no intelligible principle for the order of their experiences which they could communicate to their times. Each spent a life trying to recollect a lost vision.

So while in general, Romanticism was but one phase of a contaminated Humanism, it was in its best moments something more. It was a sense of something lost in human culture; it was a presentiment of the diminution of the human person; it was a perception of the dark side of existence beneath the spotlight of optimism; it was a dim insight into a Presence in Nature; it was the flicker of religious faith; it was the forlorn voice of the lost. This of course is not standard textbook Romanticism. However, I do believe that it represents the most vital and valuable Romanticism, for it represented a kind of foresight about the kind of world that had been in the making since the ecclesiastical condemnation pronounced in March 1277 ended the Middle Ages. It divined the fallacy of the Two Truths—the truth of Reason and the truth of Faith: there cannot be two Masters; there must be One Truth. Otherwise there is no center to hold the centrifugal forces of Humanism and the centripetal forces of Rationality in balance.

We have already seen how tight Hopkins' clerical collar was, but we now must draw up some of the deeper reasons for his ordeal. One of these was his Romantic cast of mind. It is a commonplace of Hopkins' criticism to show Hopkins as a Keatsian Romantic in his early years and then with his conversion and vocation, to insist that he become something else. Perhaps this can be put down as merely the critic's discomfort in associating Hopkins and Romanticism. It is a standard ploy of traditionalist scholars, especially Catholics, to treat Romanticism as a cultural abberration so egregious that every literary instance of it is read as "the work of the Devil." And no good can be here by definition. Nevertheless, there is a valid case for seeing Hopkins as essentially Romantic.

To begin with, Hopkins was first a poet by nature, whatever else he was by choice. This meant that he looked at life as an artist does—a vivid, concrete, personal, imaginative way. This also meant that he thought as an artist does, which is to say that his constant predilection of mind was for real rather than notional knowledge. Hopkins himself dispelled any doubt about this when he told his friend Baillie that he heartily agreed with Baillie's demurs about general rules in literary criticism, in fact every kind of generalization.[1] Further, Hopkins' strong antipathy to thinkers like Hegel indicated how competent he thought abstraction. Hopkins saw clearly that the purely notional mind was as he called it, a "bottomless pit,"[2] which can atrophy the power to maintain real commitments in life, leaving a person to the attrition of an everlasting indecision. This was the lamentable case of Hopkins' friend. E. W. Urquhart, regarding Catholicism, and Hopkins saw as much and told him so. Moreover, I think one of the main reasons Hopkins was so attracted to Newman's *Grammar of Assent* (which he admired enough to solicit more than once Newman's permission to do a commentary) was Newman's very articulate point that belief in God is not based solely on logical inferences, but primarily on real awareness of the human condition. God is a presence encountered in the reality of existence, argued Newman, and this is what makes faith. This is the very ground of being of Hopkins' poetic life.

The words, "inscape" and "instress," are now famous coinages for Hopkins' sense of reality. And when they have been stripped of their critical and philosophical baggage, are they not little more than expressions of how real knowledge comes to us? They are expressions of our seeing, feeling, contemplating, acting selves. As conceptualizations of this encounter, these terms emphasize how unique our awareness of existing things is and how unique every existing thing is. This is the knowledge of the artist; his truth is the mystery and transcendence of all existence: "It is only the poetic imagination which is akin to that of the child and the mystic that we can still feel the pure sense of mystery and transcendence which is man's natural element," wrote historian Christopher Dawson.[3]

My affirmation of this awareness as a knowledge will disturb some readers, but I see no difficulty here if it is admitted that the knowing level of the mind reaches deeply into the concrete, personal, and the preconceptual spheres of intelligence. This is to say that objective knowledge does not exhaust human knowledge. One philosopher puts it: "If the human person is aware of the presence in his consciousness of other, higher realms of being, it must mean that in some inobjective, not directly conceptualizable way, they have been grasped together with the objective aspects of an experience which can be expressed in universal concepts." This is intuitive knowledge whose primacy lies in its being ". . . personal knowledge at its highest and most perfect level, the inner grasp of another in his basic free attitude to his total world."[4] William James put it that ". . . there is in the human consciousness a sense of reality, a feeling of objective presence, a perception of what we may call 'something there,' more deep and more general than any of the special and particular senses, by which the current psychology supposes existent realities to be originally revealed. . . ."[5] It follows that for understanding of the higher levels of being, such comprehensive intuition is necessary, and in its visionary qualities this intuitive knowledge is the very source of art and religion. It is this kind of awareness which I have called the natural theology of Humanism, the intimation of which I have attributed to pure Romanticism in the guise of Wordsworth and Coleridge.

But is it at the heart of Hopkins? To say heart means his poetry, "The Windhover," for example. This famous sonnet, which has received numerous readings, seems obvious enough in its general pattern: the poet sees a falcon execute its characteristic flight maneuver with genuine delight. However, when this first response received the cutting edge of the figurations in the poem, the pattern reveals that the poet has done more than seen the bird accurately; he has in a special sense understood the bird through their encounter. If this is not true, then the sestet is merely verbal fluff and puff. But if the poet has personally and concretely seen and understood the "self" of this bird, then he has had a presentment of the whole range of existence which hints of the absolute of being. For the poet is saying that in truly encountering this bird, that is, in grasping the bird with a vital sensibility and then elevating it to the whole range of being through intuitive understanding, he has glimpsed the horizon of total being—an awesome vision. It is not surprising that the poet wants to "buckle" the bird-being to his soul, for he can "see into the life of things," a power (fire) greater (a billion times) than this splendid bird. The last three lines of the sonnet explain that it is not astonishing that the poet has come to such a grand awareness through meeting the falcon; the same shaking insights can come from any existing thing in the most prosaic of actions: sillion falling off a plow or a tiny ember off a cooling fire.

What stands out in this poem is the poet's empathic grandness of understanding, the loving grasp of real things through their natures, which is to say, their characteristic ways of coming to our sensibilities. Moreover, there is expressed the genuine feeling of awe amounting to a holy reverence which is felt when the full significance of any existing thing is truly possessed. And this response is a free getting and giving. This is to say that it constitutes a kind of faith in which one being gives to another its self-revelation freely and each is received by the other freely. The religious implications of this are obvious, and it is no wonder that Hopkins knew in his heart the real compatibility between his poetry and his religion.

If this sonnet is a fair instance of Hopkins' poetry in general, it follows that his poetic mind was essentially Romantic, for he exhibits to a rare degree those mental qualities which I have described as "pure" Romanticism—the primal mind. Poem after poem of his expresses in dramatic and graphic ways that natural theologic awareness which I have attributed to Humanism. This has been read by modern secular critics mainly along psychological lines and by many Christian readers along bluntly theological-apologetical lines. Both approaches miss the distinguishing mark of traditional Humanism which pervades Hopkins.

The by-roads modern readers have taken are readily under-

standable, for Hopkins himself has left us at a kind of inter-
section between his poetry and priesthood. It is generally accepted today that Hopkins' deepest aim was to try to harmonize
his religion, his priesthood, and his poetry. Out of this desire
came the many false starts, initiatory schemata, and fragments
which highlight his life. On this aspiration rests most of his
philosophy of art as expounded in his letters, as do most of his
critical judgments. Why did Hopkins give his life to the advocacy
of a meaningful continuity between poetry and faith?

The general answer to this question is obvious. Humanism
had lost its natural theological awareness, and thus its creativity
had no true center beyond that of refined sensibility. The logical
and as well as real result was a "realism" whose vision could not
but become nihilistic. Gradually art began to despiritualize and
thus to dehumanize. It is fair to credit Hopkins with this insight,
for his literary judgments indicate he was much aware of this
state of affairs. However, the answer in Hopkins' particular case
is not so easy to answer because on the surface it would seem
that by becoming a Catholic and then a Jesuit, he was put into
vitalizing contacts with a living tradition which still recognized
the existential base of religious faith and the consequent harmony of art and faith, culture and religion.

Maybe this is what Hopkins thought he was coming into,
but it was not the case, and the finding it out was perhaps the
tragedy of his life. Surely, it explains his deep desire to reconcile
both theoretically and personally the rift between the spiritual
and rational order of existence. He was taking on the most
formidable problem facing the modern world. His meeting of
the problem is especially meaningful because he was the problem incarnate. On the one hand he was the poet thronged with
spiritual intuitions, and on the other he chose to be the priest
yoked with promises to keep. He believed that both priest and
poet brought him to the love of God. Why then did they seem
opposed to another?

There is no easy answer to this question. And this is the proper
question, for if it is not, then Hopkins spent his intellectual and
artistic stamina with incredible blindness. Indeed, what makes
Hopkins so salient in our times is that in his life and art he

struggled valiantly to avoid living the two-faced life of modernity. This is what makes Hopkins fascinating and what makes
him so worthwhile a study.

Scholars have treated this problem in Hopkins mainly on
personal grounds. Whether it was Hopkins' Victorianism, his
Protestant conscience, his health, his confessors, or whatever
which might have caused this problem, Hopkins is assumed or
made in varying degrees to be aberrant. While I do not mean
to suggest these speculations miss the mark entirely, for they
very likely were factors, I should like to point out the possibility
that the very tradition Hopkins espoused could have been a main
factor in his difficulty—both intellectually and personally. We
know now with what affirmation, and against strong opposition,
Hopkins became a Catholic, and we know with what generosity
of heart (he destroyed what he himself considered in themselves
innocent—his poetry) he entered the Society of Jesus. Is it not
possible that the failure he considered his life to be was not
just his own personal and professional shortcomings?

I now think the answer is yes. Hopkins was taught during his
years of Jesuit training a Christian philosophical tradition which
was a confused fideism or Rationalism and thus at base, anti-
Humanistic. To what degree nineteenth-century Scholasticism
was in this disorder, I must leave to the historians of philosophy.
However, they do not leave much doubt about it. One of them,
Josef Pieper, after pointing out that immense scholarly process
of assimilating the riches of past learning which Scholasticism
was, sums up the end of the Middle Ages:

The moment had come. As bit by bit the task of acquisition was
accomplished, and as new questions demanded consideration and
answers that could only emerge from the direct experience of the
"new" peoples, mere pre-occupation with existing knowledge had
to dwindle in importance, had in the end to be seen as wide of the
mark. At the same time, by the later Middle Ages the machinery for
acquiring knowledge had been largely institutionalized. Procedures
were well established. Although they were meant primarily for ex-
ploiting existing stocks of knowledge, it was only natural for those
with a vested interest in these procedures to seek to retain them, to
continue their dominion.[6]

He then comments with the corroboration of his fellow scholars:

Ultimately that attempt could lead only to total sterility and dissolution. And that is pretty much what happened. There is no dispute
among historians on that score. The end did not descend in the form
of an external event, like the closing of the Platonic Academy by
imperial decree. Medieval philosophy degenerated from within. Grab-
mann speaks of a decay setting in precipitately. Gilson says that the
end of medieval philosophy can only be described as extreme intellectual confusion and disorder. De Wulf's general history concludes
with the statement that scholasticism died not for lack of ideas but for
lack of minds.[7]

Scholasticism was left, then, in three parts at the end of the
Middle Ages: Augustinianism, Scotism, and Thomism. Various
religious orders espoused one of these as their theological format.
This meant that the tradition of Christian philosophy had a
spectrum of disarray going from Augustinism with its strong
suspicion of reason, through Scotism with its predilection for
fideism, to Thomism with its flirtation with Rationalism. While
theoretically, it was Rationalism which the Condemnation of
1277 squelched in the name of the Augustinian tradition, it
was this very Rationalism in the guise of science which, in the
long protracted confusion of the Christian intellectual tradition,
has come to dominate knowledge. The resurrection of Thomas
Aquinas in the nineteenth century and his virtual domination
of modern Christian thought is oblique testimony to the insight
of the Medieval Church about the danger of Scholasticism. Josef
Pieper puts it: "From the beginning medieval scholasticism was
threatened by an internal peril, one arising from the very nature
of its tenets. The peril can be summed up in a single word:
rationalism. It was necessary to keep this in bounds."[8] Neo-
Thomists today would not dub St. Thomas a Rationalist, and
however good their arguments, their very denial exhibits that
vacillation of Christian thought since the 1277 Condemnation
occasioned the philosophical controversy which ended the Middle
Ages. For as Gilson points out, "The center around which the
controversy will revolve is Thomism itself as seen from the
different point of views of his supporters and of its opponents."[9]

The Society of Jesus, of course, soon founded its machinery of learning and before long entered the lists of Christian thought. Relevant to our interests is the sixteenth-century Jesuit theologian, Francisco Suarez, who tried to make a kind of *summa* of the confusion and disorder which Gilson says that Scholasticism became. Possessed of a brilliantly juridical mind, Suarez drew up in a legalist manner an eclectic compendium of Scholasticism which had obvious instructional merits for the Society and thus became a teaching guide through the shoals of Christian teaching. Now it was Suarez which Hopkins was taught during his Jesuit training days, and it is clear that Suarez was not satisfactory to Hopkins. It must be remembered that Hopkins had read in the Classical philosophers during his Oxford days—Aristotle and Plato being his favorites. When he entered the Society and was put through a program of Scholastic philosophy, Suarez was his only contact with the heritage of medieval Scholasticism. He apparently had little firsthand acquaintance with St. Thomas. So he was taught a hybrid scholasticism which did not engage him, and in his distraction, he came upon Scotus and found "philosophical salvation." This did not please his Jesuit mentors, and despite his hopes as well as his Oxford qualification, he was not promoted to a further year of theological studies, thus closing the way to him for a professorship with the Society.

The question is why the turn from Suarez and the taking up of Scotus. After all, Hopkins was an amateur in Scholasticism. I think a hint of an explanation lies in some remarks Hopkins made about Jesuit theologians: "Suarez is our most famous theologian: he is a man of vast volume of mind, but without originality or brilliancy; he treats everything satisfactorily, but you never remember a phrase of his, the manner is nothing. Molina is the man who *made* our theology: he was a genius and even in his driest dialect I have remarked a certain fervour like a poet's."[10]

". . . a certain fervour like a poet's." Here is our hint. Hopkins found no grounds in Suarez' legalisms for his Romantic vision of reality, that is to say what I have called his Christian Humanism. This would be an understandable reaction of a poet to philosophical disquisition in general, but it must be remembered that

Hopkins brought with him high hopes of finding a continuity between his artistic and his religious life. There was an intimate alliance in him of imagination and piety based on what must be called his sense of the real, and thus any philosophy which did not give a reasonable account of this reality, the very core of his life, art, religion, and vocation, simply would not do. It also must be remembered what bias Hopkins must have felt in the attitude of the Society which had a long tradition of antipathy toward poetry, which, as W. H. Gardner has pointed out, ". . . since the days of *Poeticae Institutiones* of Jacobus Pontanus (d. 1628), who laid down that poetry is justified only in so far as it promotes virtue; that all passion and self must be suppressed; and that poetry is allowed at all only as a concession to the fallen condition of human nature, which is not strong enough to endure the nakedness and severity of eternal truth."[11] Now Hopkins knew this even in his lessened rigor in his own time. How could he help not finding the very demands of his high calling in direct conflict with his very self? It may very well be that he saw an opportunity to change the traditional attitude of his Society, or at least he toyed with the idea despite the fear and trembling of his conscience. Whatever else, he could not help being a poet and thus writing poetry, for he ". . . *loved* the children of his muse. . . ."[12]

I believe Professor Gardner is right about Hopkins' basic conviction in this matter: "But although for him the Good (what pleases us) is not necessarily the Right (what is *morally* good), he was loath to divorce Beauty from Truth."[13] It follows from this that Hopkins must have found in Scotus some philosophical possibility for holding these together. The turn to Scotus has many significances, then. In this event, there is surfaced the problem of Hopkins' art (the survival in a Rationalist's milieu of Christian Humanism in the guise of Romanticism); the problem of his religion (the assent to the presence of God in real experience); the problem of his vocation (the Jesuit quarrel with poetry); the problem of Humanism (one Truth or many truths).

What did Scotus have to offer? In my opinion, he provided a theological key to make Hopkins' Romanticism consonant with

Christianity. At least Hopkins thought so. That key is the Scotist concept of the "self." On this Hopkins is able to found his own notions of his experience—inscape and instress. He is able to find theological assurance for his notion of the Heroic Self of Christ. And he is able to link his poetic sense of man with the Christian idea of grace. What he left us is at most a schema, but nevertheless there is enough to see how he thought he might have put together a solution to his problems—personal, poetic, and religious.

In going from Suarez to Scotus, there is some need to understand along general Scholastic lines what this meant. It meant going from a tendentious version of a la mode Scholastic to an out and out "negative theologian," that is to say, to a thinker possessed of a clearly reasoned insight that knowledge of God infinitely exceeds the range of human understanding. Pieper calls this a ". . . fundamental corrective of all possible rationalism. . . ."[14] Yes, but it can be asked: Was Suarez in any sense a Rationalist? Yes, he was, for according to Josef Pieper, there emerged a "new Rationalism" at the breakup of the Middle Ages. This took the form of reducing philosophizing to a purely historical examination of philosophical questions as construed by various thinkers. Pieper asserts that this brings about two most unfortunate results. First, the focus of philosophy is shifted from the meaning and structure of the real world to the logicalities of philosophers; second, philosophy becomes lost in the forest of historical facticity. This emasculates philosophy as St. Thomas, whom he quotes, insisted: "The purpose of the study of philosophy is not to learn what others have thought, but to learn how the truth of things stand."[15] To my mind, while there are good and valid reasons for paying attention to the historical traditions of thought, this form of Rationalism has continued to petrify the Scholastic tradition until our own times. In making Suarez one kind of Rationalist, perhaps I am being inaccurate; however, there is no doubt that Hopkins, for whom being earnest for reality was a touchstone of all thought and art,[16] Suarez was out of touch. Moreover, it is significant that Scotus is looked upon by one historian of philosophy as correcting the "rational optimism" of St. Thomas, and most consider Scotus far more negative than Aquinas about the possible conjunction of reason and faith.[17]

I have said "self" is the key because Hopkins was convinced that the truth of things lay in singular existence, and that through their concrete and unique presence to the mind, an intuitive knowledge elevates the awareness of a limited singular existent to some discernment of total and thus absolute Being. The personal character of this knowledge together with its awesome heights normally results in a sense of witness, of having seen, with profound affective overtones of religious commitment—faith. Thus "self" was the keystone to Hopkins' real order of existence and out of it came his faith and his art. Now I will leave it to Scotus specialists whether Hopkins had found in Scotus a real counterpart to his notion of "self." Father Christopher Devlin, whom I consider to have done definitive work on this matter, shows clearly where Hopkins found counterparts in Scotus, and in general legitimately so, for his "inscapes."[18]

But it was a *theological* key Hopkins was ultimately seeking, one which would reconcile his religion and his art. Of course, he had gone a long way in finding affirmation for his sense of "self" and toward validating his own artistic and religious experience, for he had found reasons in one of the great Christian traditionalists for keeping Beauty and Goodness together. One way of putting this is to say that Scotus gave Hopkins reasons for attributing to the imagination an intellective capacity to know truth in a very special way—intuitively, comprehensively, yet personally and concretely.[19] This amounts to the insight which I have called the natural theology of Humanism and the "pure" Romanticism of Wordsworth and Coleridge. What was taken for granted in the Christian Humanism of the Renaissance has here become the very issue of Humanism for a devout Christian. The union between intellect and sense which Scotus insists upon can be looked on as an intellective imagination in whose "vision of existence" there lies some of the truth of things. Thus there is another kind of knowing which brings us into the life of reality: Beauty can be the way of Truth. As Hopkins tartly and trenchantly put it in a comment on Hell in his spiritual writings: "This simple explanation will never strike our scholastics, because they do not see that there is an intellectual imagination."[20] Perhaps not some contemporary Scholastics, but Coleridge very likely would have understood what he meant.

This primary intuition of real experience was the basis of Hopkins' religious faith, and Scotus' rationale, while a heartening support after Suarez, offered much more to Hopkins than a grammar of assent. Newman, whose expression this is, could well have provided this. Scotus provided a theological frame which Hopkins found fruitfully suggestive to his own speculations. Perhaps a question might be asked to open up just in what way Hopkins found Scotus most helpful theologically. In what way does the finite "self," trailing its wisps of Infinity, communicate the Christian Trinity? This is another way of asking about the relation between the assent of faith and the contents of belief. The question went to the heart of the matter for Hopkins both as poet and a Christian. Was it possible that the "inscapes" Hopkins perceived were in some way "inscapes" of Christ?

Actually, the speculations in attempting to answer this question are built on one of Hopkins' early notions, that of "instress." It will be remembered that "stress" was the name of the forces which existents are. When an existent "stresses" a mind and is received, that is, the mind apprehends the nature of object-self (instress), there occurs an "inscape." The subject-self glimpses the form of the object-self. Stress, then, is the being-power through which individuals communicate on some level. Thus the question before Hopkins was how does this being-power become spiritual energy caused by and in cooperation with God's creative power? The answer which Hopkins gave was the Incarnation. But how does Christ relate to Divinity "selving" Nature? This is what Hopkins was after. It meant a reworking of the theology of the Trinity, which Hopkins did, with Scotus leading the way.

Hopkins did not see Christ's descent into creation as primarily reparative, but rather he held that it was an act of love pre-destined whether there had been sin or not. The act of love constituted God's performance of an act of an inferior nature, an aspect of love not possible to him as God alone. So from eternity God willed to express this aspect of love—God the Son's descent into creation. Hopkins' thought was confirmed in

Duns Scotus, who taught this. This "great sacrifice," as Hopkins called it, became the *theological* key because in this view creation depended upon the Incarnation, rather than the reverse which many theologians held. Now the encounter of the "self" becomes in a theological sense the glimpsed form of the "Divine Self" behind Nature-Christ-scapes. Father Devlin puts it that Christ's human nature is the perfect image of the Divine Essence, and as the predestined before all creatures, He is the head of the human race as well as all the lower levels contained in human nature—elemental, vegetative, and sensitive. "From this it would seem to follow that all the multitudinous degrees of perfection in created things combine like some mathematical formula to express the intrinsic degree of Christ's created perfection." Father Devlin adds, "Indeed mathematical or musical terms would be better than logical ones to describe this mystical unity."[21] Here is the clue to the special attraction Scotus had for Hopkins. His identity with Scotus' theology of the Incarnation, which Father Devlin thinks central, laid the theological basis for holding Beauty and Goodness together, for making poems which went from expressing the presence of God's inscape in animate nature ("The Windhover") to the working out of that design in the stress and instress of the hearts of men ("The Wreck of the Deutschland" and the "terrible" sonnets). Well we can wonder whether Hopkins would have written his poetry without Scotus, "He . . . who of all men most sways my spirits to peace. . . ."[22] Perhaps Hopkins had an intimation when he first came on Scotus that though hidden and halting, he could go on being a poet as a priest: "At this time I had first begun to get hold of the copy of Scotus on the Sentences in the Baddely library and was flush with a new stroke of enthusiasm. It may come to nothing or it may be a mercy from God. But just then when I took in any inscape of the sky or sea I thought of Scotus."[23]

In suggesting this "poetic salvation" for Hopkins, I make Hopkins all the more enigmatic, for in considering the depreciative way Hopkins treated his poetry in public (Father Devlin to my mind is excessive in his image of the slut and her children), I do not find beyond any doubt that Scotus really solved Hopkins' problems. To be sure, he felt less restrained in denying his poetic genius; in his spare time, he could do some writing. The great irony is that despite his enormous enthusiasm for Scotus, whose great watchword was *freedom* of God and man, Hopkins was able to let go heedless obvious guides to reconciling his own choices and desires (the case is compounded with St. Ignatius, whose spiritual advice amounted to a prudent recognition of his poetic nature). Father Devlin attributes to Hopkins' attitudes three possible elements: vanity of self-esteem, Calvinistic Victorianism, and a psychological error about desire and choice. For myself, I would choose vanity of self-esteem, and I choose to think that Hopkins knew himself all too well from the beginning. Two years before he thought about the priesthood and virtually a year before his conversion he wrote in his diary: "On this day by God's grace I resolved to give up all beauty until I had His leave for it. . . ."[24] Though he struggled against himself a lifetime and the trail of his battle has become a glorious one, Hopkins never thought "His leave" had been given him despite the fact that he wished for it so very much. What was worse, he had given in to his nature many times: there were the children of his muse! Did he have to slaughter the innocents again? No, not literally, but he had to destroy his self-devotion in his poems, "an instressing of his own inscape," which was what Lucifer did. Near the end of his life, in what must have been an agonizing and excruciating resolution, he brought himself to a degree of detachment which satisfied his conscience. He then resigned his poems to God's care. Scotus would have understood this culmination: he held that the love of beauty was an initial impulse to the love of God.[25]

Professor Gardner wrote of Hopkins' concentration and brilliant elaboration of the unique "selfs" of existence: "It has not been sufficiently stressed that his preoccupation with the individual, the *self*, was a Romantic trait stemming from Hazlitt and Keats."[26] The Romantic traits I have been trying to exhibit come more from the first generation Romantics where I believe there still exist some of the insights of the natural theology of Humanism. I hold that Hopkins provided a radical corrective to the decadence of self which Romanticism had become in his time, for he gave it a deific center out of which could come again some grand transcendental values and perspectives. Thus Romanticism more than regained that grasp and reach of poetic power and insight we briefly read in Wordsworth and Coleridge. In Hopkins' Christian Romanticism, the world and man again begin to take on that monumentality we associate with the Renaissance and before that with Hellenism—creation and cosmos. Here is where Hopkins and Pater come together.

II

To say that Pater was a modernist is to place him intellectually ahead of his times as was Hopkins similarly advanced in poetry. Since Hopkins was generally traditional and orthodox in his own thinking, their minds would seem to be poles apart. After all Hopkins stood for metaphysics, sacred history, Catholic orthodoxy, and religious obedience. These imply stances of mind and modes of experience which any clear-thinking modernist would have to question. And Pater did challenge them.

The received mode of thinking and feeling, which is tradition, Pater believed to be in dissolution. He believed what was called for was a fresh renewal of humanism through the aegis of the two most powerfully shaping spirits of Western culture—Hellenism and Christianity. In his time, he believed, that this could be done if certain principal awarenesses were heeded. The first of these was fundamental: the willingness to re-examine ruthlessly tradition itself. To do this meant to have doubt in the face of time-sanctified absolutes and to assume that the possibility of change was to be charged with relativism. Pater accepted this burden forthrightly: "Modern thought is distinguished from ancient by its cultivation of the 'relative' spirit in the place of the 'absolute.'"[27] Pater meant by this that modern thought was experimental, that the locus of truth was individual and concrete, that knowing was both generalizing and concretizing.

Though this spirit was a modern emphasis, Pater held that it has always been the true stance of the mind. He believed that these qualities have always been the attributes of great-minded cultures and the distiguishing marks of genius. The greatest example to him was Plato, who possessed to an extraordinary degree this temper of mind: "For him, all gifts of sense and intelligence converge in one supreme faculty of theoretic vision, *Oewpia*, the imaginative reason."[28] This is to say that Plato had powerful capacity to carry sense complexes to the level of mental abstractions. His universals thus were expressed through the created concretions of his imagination with their powerful attachments to the real world. Pater is saying that Plato is a supreme example of speculative thought in which there is imaginative creativity, aesthetic qualities, and figurative expression. Truth is thus tempered by the mind that possesses it because the mind itself is a real element partly creating what it perceives. This creativity is what constitutes the special genius of any great thinker.

The "relative spirit" of the modern mind, then, acknowledges the subjective aspects of thought and therefore understands that all truth is incomplete. Every mode of thinking and every system of thought has a certain relativity, which is to say that it is able to be modified by further enlightenments of fresh genius. This view also notes that permanent human experiences are freshly perceived by each man in his time, for this *present* awareness constitutes his reality. Not only are impressions subject to the perpetual flight of time and mental enervation, but also every impression ". . . is the impression of an individual in his isolation, each mind keeping as a solitary prisoner its own dream of a world." All of this bears heavily on what we call tradition, for from one point of view of the mind, tradition is a complex of mentalities; from another, that of history, tradition is a process of diverse mental forces actively entering into the shapes and movements of things.

It follows thus that tradition is a human process in which every level of existence has some part to play. Pater asserted:

. . . the essence of humanism is that belief . . . that nothing which has ever interested living men and women can wholly lose its vitality— no language they have spoken, nor oracle beside which they have hushed their voices, no dream which has once been entertained by actual human minds, nothing about which they have ever been passionate, or expended time or zeal.[29]

Moreover, total history disallows any final and unalterable history because both the integrating mind and the corpus of facts are limited and incomplete. Pater insisted: "The humanist, he who possesses the complete culture, does not weep over the failure of a theory of qualification of the predicate, nor shriek over the fall of a philosophical formula."[30]

Tradition then is a quality of mind enacted in time. To procure insights into tradition requires a careful estimate of the historical complex and the play of the human mind, especially the creative forces of genius. This meant that the shape of any era was stamped by the human spirit, and only by discovering where the key alliances were formed between the creative personalities of genius and the circumstances of their times, can we understand and learn from tradition. For tradition is a series of "elevated points" of human achievement whose spirit lives on in succeeding cultures and generations, a very long time if it has been brilliantly and powerfully forged in its inception—Greece, for example. Moreover, while time can bring any culture to extinction, it is possible to uncover its buried spirit through recovery of its genius by means of the very mode which produces the great tradition: the humanistic spirit. Nineteenth-century man needed to rediscover the true temper of this Humanism, in Pater's judgment best exemplified on Hellenism, if the details of modern life were ever to satisfy the human spirit.

This basically is what Pater is all about—to rescue the human person from what he called, ". . . the fatal, irresistible, mechanic play of circumstance. . . ."[31] If this is true, then Pater was a very special kind of modernist, for while he generally accepted the modes of the experimental mind, he made a distinction between personality and facts which most experimentalists seldom ponder. The distinction arises from his consideration of what scientists take for granted: order and the mind. They can take these as given because their very methods account for certain predispositions about both—the infinite extension of order and the problematical state of the mind. Pater saw and appreciated the value of such a mentality in the study of the natural order wherein physical causality yields its secrets to such inquiry. But when this method is turned upon the human complex, a great and telling imponderable is confronted: the personality. To ignore the creative capacities of the human personality meant to dehumanize culture, and Pater judged that this is what precisely confronted his time. To counteract this, he tried to combine scientific with Humanistic attitudes. In both his *Renaissance* and *Plato and Platonism*, he tried to use history scientifically, which is to say constructurally, and at the same time delineate personality as it met its circumstances with its special creative forces. Pater has often been accused of not being much of a scholar, mainly, I think, because he refused to assume that the experimental methods of physical science applied univocally to social science.

This meant basically that the relationship assumed by physical scientists between the mind and order was not the same as that assumed by the Humanists. This was the second principal awareness which Pater thought essential to a renewal of culture. What Pater was insisting upon is that the kind of knowledge which scientists possess is but one kind of knowing, a kind which perhaps best serves the objective physical world; there is another kind of knowing, which might be called the dialectic of self, through which men come to greater awareness of the spiritual springs of human existence. And the characteristics of this knowledge are in contrast with those of science. Where the scientist observes, the humanist experiences; where the scientist constructs, the humanist knows intuitively; where the scientist theorizes, the humanist envisions; where the scientist possesses his solving concept, the humanist possesses his "selving" contemplation. Pater's "imaginative reason," then, was an attempt to yoke together these two great mental powers into a union which might tap the wellspring of the human spirit. He argued that it was just such a conjunction of human powers which produced the greatest era of Humanism in Western culture—Greece, and he asserted that the greatest example to his times was the father of this spirit—Plato.

And how is this special temper of mind loosed as an active force? Primarily through an aesthetic means. In the case of Plato, it was the dialogue which Pater thought possessed just the right combination of rational and imaginative qualities to express this mind—the dramatic enactment of the mind self-reflecting to a point of definition. Very unlike the formal treatise, which Pater thought to be the philosophical counterpart to the scientific demonstration, ". . . native intuition shrunk into dogmatic system, the dry bones of which rattle in one's ears, with Aristotle, or Aquinas, or Spinoza . . . ,"[32] the dialogue represented the perfect literary form of philosophic expression. Beginning in real experience, staying in close touch with their affective images through the power of the imagination, the dialogue was a dramatic poem enacting the birth of an idea. And like all ideas in poems, their order of existence is the artistic form of the expressive structure. This is to say that truth and the mind are an interpersonal relationship of the mind and its uniquely expressive creations. Thus Pater insisted upon the real experience of encounter in knowing, the sense of *person* in knowledge, and while he agrees that Plato is seeking nothing less than absolute truth,

Yet, in spite of all that, in spite of the demand he makes for certainty and exactness and what is absolute, in all real knowledge, he does think, or inclines his reader to think, that truth, precisely because it resembles some high kind of relationship of persons to persons, depends a good deal on the receiver; and must be, in that degree, elusive, provisional, contingent, a matter of various approximation, and of an "economy," as is said; that it is partly a subjective attitude of mind:—that philosophic truth consists in the philosophic temper.[33]

This is the dialectical method according to Pater. It follows that Platonism is the translating of the Platonic dialogue into a formal philosophical treatise, making what was a contemplative vision a rational doctrine. While Pater admits that the formal treatise is one of the literary forms of philosophy, he makes it very clear that in his opinion this form tends to make the philosophic mind effete. The result was a doctrinaire Rationalism which extended from Aristotle to Spinoza and which was in danger of becoming even more categorical under the pressures of scientific thought in his own time. Thus the very spirit whose purpose was to startle the apprehension into greater awareness

of the spiritual depths and riches of real experience in the thicket
of personal life was busy editing experience to fit categories.
Very likely this seems an ungenerous and exaggerated rebuke of
some very great minds; it better fits their commentators. Still
it is Pater's judgment that the philosophic temper in his day was
sickly and desperately needed some new and vigorous exercises
rather than being kept in bed by the old doctors. It would not be
long before the scientists would come in to administer drugs.

I believe there is a clear and instructive parallel between
Pater's Humanism and Hopkins' Christian Romanticism. First,
there is a fundamental relation between the kind of knowing
Hopkins appreciated so intensely in Scotus, what was called
"visio existentis," and what Pater admired in Plato as the mind
of the true Humanist, the "imaginative reason." In both, a clear
distinction is held between the real and notional levels of knowing; both are visionary of something existing; they seek to give
certainty and meaning to the pattern of sensation; they, being
preconscious, plumb the unconscious mind; they journey to
glimpse the infinite; both, though prior to distinct knowing,
attempt to unite intellect and senses; while a real union is
achieved between subject and object in both, neither vision nor
imaginative reason have present in them the inmost self of the
existent and thus in a certain sense each is tentative and confused, yet the soul rejoices in its receivership of Being. What I
should like to stress here is that both Hopkins and Pater were
trying to formulate a knowing process which would validate the
kind of apprehension of experience which produces art and religion. Evidently, this would be different from the abstractive
intellect of either science or metaphysics, though not unrelated.

Moreover, there is a basic likeness between Hopkins' "inscape"
and Pater's "philosophic temper." As we have seen, Hopkins
found Scotus' explanation of encounter with Nature highly compatible with his own thought and experience, for Hopkins believed that he experienced some special tension between himself
and things, what he called *stress*, to which he responded generously with all his faculties—his own self—which he called
instress. The resultant union was *inscape* in which he glimpsed
the unique form of the being present to him bringing him a fleet-

ing awareness of Divinity "selving" Nature. Presences encounter presences in a personal, concrete, and real awareness; presences greet presences in dialogue. Is this not what Pater understands to be the philosophic temper? Truth, he said, ". . . resembles some high kind of relationship of persons to persons. . . ." Later, he noted that truth ". . . is a partly subjective state of mind. . . ." Is not Hopkins' counterpart *instress*, the subject's answer to the object dealing out itself and without which response there is no *inscape*, no meeting and greeting?

I think that the parallel is clear, and it is significant because the similarity of response to their times between two sensitive and intelligent Victorians of modernist and orthodox views suggests that the nineteenth century was trapped between tradition and modernity—an awareness that Matthew Arnold felt acutely. Tradition had come to mean a closed mind; modernity seemed to mean an uncloseable mind. Both Hopkins and Pater judged that neither stance adequately fostered the human spirit, and each judged from inside, deeply inside, the traditionalist and the modernist position. For Hopkins did turn away from the Scholastic Rationalism he was taught as a Jesuit and sought a philosophic view more compatible with his poetic personality, more explanatory of his religious experience, which is to say, more realistic, less Rationalistic. And Pater was not satisfied with the scientific thinking which his fellow modernists were espousing; rather he sought to locate the kind of rational spirit which fostered a truly Humanistic culture. He saw that science was not studying that which makes man free, but that which binds him. Both Hopkins and Pater knew that man does not perfect himself by authoritarian arguments or demonstrated theories, but by his capacity to spiritualize his experience.

Hopkins tried very hard to relocate his deep commitment to the Christian tradition, first by his conversion and then by searching back through Catholic tradition for a more existential view than he had been introduced to in his Jesuit education. That he found philosophical solace in the Middle Ages is not surprising, for Scholasticism then was richly individual and undoctrinaire, a quality of that spirit which the subsequent tradition had successfully diminished. Hopkins, of course, was not committing apostasy by taking up Scotus and using him as a guide in theological and philosophical matters and he knew it. Still he was countering the Church's counsel that St. Thomas be the model in such matters. That he went far another way is brilliantly shown in the blueprint of his speculations we have been left in his spiritual writings.

Moreover, I suggest that Hopkins was seeking to give spiritual value to his imaginative world and some poetic value to his spiritual life. Both values had long been dissociated with art and religion except in rare circumstances. They are a consequence of that general dissociation of sensibility of which T. S. Eliot has remarked. Thus art and religion themselves increasingly lost any intersubjectivity. Hopkins in his own religious and artistic life keenly felt this depreciation, and in both he labored to redress the stuation. His Christian Romanticism stands as his judgment and his achievement.

Pater also sought a different way. While Hopkins was content to go back into the tradition he espoused and find fresh incentive, in some sense Pater's road was more difficult, for he found it harder to ignore Christian tradition in order to go back into the pagan. This was not just because of the long ascendancy of Christianity, but because Pater was a religious man, and as Lord Cecil noted, "Religion with Pater meant the Christian religion."[34] There are those who would argue that Hopkins' tradition was holiness and Pater's beauty; however, their lives and their works belie these categories. Both were really seeking the same goals of the good and the beautiful which ever led the way.

Nevertheless, Pater cleared the ground of nettles and barriers of orthodoxy, and as we have seen, began to work out his own approach to the renewal of culture. The ground clearing took place, for the most part, in his early essays, but his first positive step was his book on the Renaissance. That Pater chose to treat this period is significant because it suggests that his often sharp arguments against the Christianity of his day were dissatisfactions with the then current expressions of Christian culture rather than with essential Christianity. If he wished to renew pure Hellenism, surely he would not have chosen the Renaissance, which represents a richly Christian era newly meeting a resurrected Classicism and getting along rather famously. It is not surprising to find that this is why he chose this historical period. It is even more notable that he decided that there were things there to be learned which his times needed.

The keynote to the Renaissance for Pater is an "outbreak of the human spirit." He finds medieval France already possessing its central characteristics: ". . . the care for physical beauty, the worship of the body, the breaking down of those limits which the religious system of the middle age imposed on the heart and on the imagination." Not only these attractively Humanistic qualities merit frequent study, but also its ". . . general spirit and character, for the ethical qualities of which it is the consummate type." Pater thought that the Renaissance culminated in France in the middle of the sixteenth century, though its spirit protracted a long, drawnout vanishment, ". . . the products of which have to the full that subtle and delicate sweetness which belongs to a refined and comely decadence, just as its earliest phases have the freshness which belongs to all periods of growth in art, the charm of *ascesis*, of the austere and serious girding of the lions of youth." The last essay (on Winckelmann) remarks on the close of the Renaissance, a brilliant flourish before its extinction in the eighteenth century, ". . . the last fruit of the Renaissance, and explains in a striking way its motives and tendencies."[35]

Pater insists that the Renaissance is an amalgam of pagan Humanism and the Christian faith. Therefore, a rather standard claim that the Renaissance spirit was opposed to Christian culture is, in Pater's understanding of the circumstances and events, largely false. Indeed in the medieval Renaissance which he takes up in the first essay, he notes that to depict the Middle Ages as an "age of faith" is misleading. Pater finds this middle period antinomial in that there is such a clear manifestation of sense pleasure and the imagination, beauty and the body, which clearly went against the Christian ideal ". . . and their love became sometimes a strange idolatry, a strange rival religion." This can be seen in Abelard, echoed in Dante, exemplified in the legend of Tannhäuser and "Li Amitiez de Ami et Amile," made famous in the story of *Aucassin and Nicolette*.

The Renaissance, then, is more than a revival of Classical antiquity:

For us the Renaissance is the name of a many-sided but yet united movement, in which the love of the intellect and the imagination for their own sake, the desire for a more liberal and comely way of conceiving life, make themselves felt, urging those who experience this desire to search out first one and then another means of intellectual or imaginative enjoyment, and directing them not only to the discovery of old and forgotten sources of this enjoyment, but to the divination of fresh sources thereof—new experiences, new subjects of poetry, new forms of art.[36]

It is Pater's argument that this spirit cuts across a whole complex of tendencies and motives, some of which are born of the long development of Christianity and some of which are the surfacing of even older cultures. To Pater, a plethora of circumstances and conditions turned the Middle Ages to ". . . sweetness; and the taste for sweetness generated there becomes the seed of classical revival in it, prompting it constantly to seek after the springs of perfect sweetness in the Hellenic world."

It is this reading of the history of Renaissance Humanism that is central to Pater's general idea of the development of the highest achievement in Western culture, the clue to any further possibilities of advance in his own time, and the kind of mentality necessary to any sort of integration of the modern mind. The grand works of Greece had to be appreciated as the great aboriginal of Western Humanism, and no human and humane attainments in the same class of monumentality can be reached for without heeding their splendid work. In the Renaissance, this meant reconciling Apollo and Christ, for these had been the two elemental forces shaping Western history. This work was barely begun during the Renaissance in fifteenth-century Italy and rather badly so. Still it was initiated at this time though, according to Pater, the main accomplishments were to be done in the Enlightenment and in his own time. It is not too much to say that he saw this as one of his main endeavors.

Pater notes that it was Pico della Mirandola who began early to wonder "whether the religion of Greece was indeed a rival

of the religion of Christ . . . ,"[37] not with what Pater called the
historic sense of his own day, but rather with what he called,
". . . the leading instinct, the curiosity, the initiatory idea."[38]
Essentially this idea was a sense of the relation of the past, a
feeling for all that has ever interested the human mind, even
though whatever reconciliation attempted between paganism
and Christianity was by way of allegory. Pater thought Pico's
life and work represented the true Humanist of the Italian
Renaissance. It was his generous response to both the sacred and
profane traditions of Western culture, the mixing of the two in
art and thought, which Pater thought was the real significance
of Pico's life. He embodied this defining quality of the Renaissance in Italy, a quality of Humanism which highlights the best
art of this time.

However, Pico's Humanism was more than a general curiosity
over vestiges; his care was the magnificence of man. Pater
quotes Thomas More's description of Plato to show that excellence of mind was matched by bodily beauty, and in recounting
his life stresses Pico's oration on the dignity of human nature.
Pater saw this emphasis as a "counterpoise to the increasing
tendency of medieval religion to depreciate man's nature, to
sacrifice this or that element in it, to make it ashamed of itself,
to keep the degrading or painful accidents of it always in view."
The Renaissance, then, was a rehabilitation of human nature
in all its fullness.

This is another way of saying that medieval Christianity
needed a Humanistic counterbalance to its supernaturalism.
Pater understood the Italian Renaissance to have begun this
readjustment. He cited instance after instance in his study of
the mixture and fusion of pagan and Christian motives in the
minds and art of the great Italian artists in the fifteenth century.
However, it is in the essay on Winckelmann that he stated
rather completely his view of Western tradition. While Pater is
concerned in his study to isolate the peculiar temper of this
eighteenth-century Hellenist, he offers the kind of comprehensive awareness he thinks necessary to appreciate the development of Western civilization and to know where to seek its revival
in his own times.

The first point Pater has to make is that Apollo and Christ are out of their tombs and have been encountering each other over and over again in the minds and hearts of men. Even though men look at the marvelous manifestations of this meeting, Raphael's frescoes in the Vatican, for example, they do not seem to realize an organic development of human culture, but rather some sort of paralleling of the old and the true. This is Pater's second point: the past lives in the present; Greek artistic orthodoxy is made to express Christian culture. He could have gone on to observe that this was the result of medievalism, for one of the distinctive marks of this age was to find counterparts between paganism and Christianity, and while the ordeal of this endeavor on the intellectual plane is well known, too little is appreciated of the general accord that came about between Classical art and the Christian spirit—though as Pater says, it is before our very eyes.

Perhaps Pater had the explanation for the comparative ease with which Greek art fused with the Christian religion: "Out of Greek religion, under happy circumstances, arises Greek art, to minister to human culture."[39] The ability of Greek religion to be transformed into an artist's ideal was due to the fact that its deific quality was the human form and spirit made magnificent. It possessed, therefore, the greatest readiness to universalize and make visible the human condition. This potentiality of expressiveness enabled the Greek religious spirit to be heightened powerfully through artistic form. Moreover, the widest range of imaginative speculation about human life was fused with religious modes of experience in the great crossroads of Greek art. Pater noted this dividing difference between Greek and Christian religion: "For the thoughts of Greeks about themselves, and their relation to the world generally, were ever in the happiest readiness to be transformed into objects of the senses. In this lies the main distinction between Greek art and the mystical art of the Christian middle age, which is always struggling to express thoughts beyond itself."[40] Here Pater hit a key point about culture which I believe has been raised today to the level of a general social truth: culture is leavened by religion.[41] When this leavening occurs richly, as in Greece, there results an immensely fruitful and elevated Humanistic spirit, Humanistic because Greek religion ministered to man, spiritualized him in a very special sense.

What about Christianity then? Has it ever produced such a culture, and inevitably, what relation does it have with the Hellenic? This is what Pater's book is all about. He answered the question in the affirmative—citing the Renaissance. He noted how the Humanistic elements of the Christian religion began to be brought out through the Greek tradition of art and how, as a result, Christian art began to have the powerful monumentality of the Hellenic world. But there is a side to Christianity which condemns this spirit of Humanism in religion, a side which wants the world to be hung in the crepe of its nether nature, a side which finds in every beauty the bugs of silent ravishment. This spirit produces the culture of specter-man, silent and guilty. It looks away from art and thus loses the voice of its soul.

All things are mediated in and through art. This, says Pater, is the key to Greece: "In its poets and orators, its historians and philosophers, Greece cannot be conceived from a central point, unless one brings, as a key to understanding of it, an insight into the ideal forms of sculpture, and regards the images of statesmen and philosophers, as well as epic and dramatic heroes, from the artistic point of view."[42] That is, if religion is the content of culture, then art is its form. No system of thought, no mode of feeling, no thicket of experience derives its total value from some abstracted objectivity, for the existential is as much created as perceived. Moreover, the highest spirit of the mind, the philosophic, has its genius in its envisioning and expressive powers and not in its high-powered hypothetical absolutes, because the gamut of human dimensions is contained in art and there specified, identified, and memorialized—is made human in a splendid way.

So to Pater, the Renaissance was a breaking out of the human spirit once more because man had begun to freshly rediscover himself. This led inevitably to the first great epiphany of man. Once again Greek breadth, centrality, blitheness, and repose— all of those marks of man in unity with himself, his physical nature and the outward world, beamed into the pale faces of the followers of Christ. Pater's view of medievalism partook of the still prevalent historical bias, "gothic medievalism." It is clear that to him medievalism found little in the human personality beyond that of being fallen and deprived. To be sure, there was an enormous concentration on the human capacity for spiritualization, the special virtues of the time, but Pater did not see much significance for the self in their spirit. This is another another way of saying that human creativity, human value, seemed to have relatively little significance in the Middle Ages, and therefore Humanism and its once glorious accomplishment would be despirited as long as men ignored the dignity and prowess that even medievalists granted that man possessed.

Yet Pater made a considerable departure from this historical cliche. Perhaps his very method of drawing up the chief circumstances of an age and locating where personal genius confronted predicaments with creative power, prevented any such easy view. In his essay on Winckelmann, Pater notes that there was in the Greek spirit an element of conflict, an ennui, eventually an overpowering rival claim best expressed in Greek tragedy. After all, Godlike man was not a god, but the tragic form could enact how like a god he could suffer, being a man. The grief of disharmony in existence Pater saw as elemental in Greek religion and premonitory to medievalism:

Around the feet of that tranquil Olympian family still crowd the weary shadows of an earlier, more formless, divine world. The placid minds even of Olympian gods are troubled with thoughts of a limit to duration, of inevitable decay, of dispossession. Again, the supreme and colourless abstraction of those divine forms, which is the secret of their repose, is also a premonition of the fleshless, consumptive refinements of the pale, medieval artists.[43]

However, according to Pater, the decline of the artistic sense in the interest of asceticism laid the basis for an even more intense reassertion of its claims when the world came into the Church and burst into life again—the Renaissance.

What Pater is arguing against is any sort of absolute division between medieval and Renaissance culture. He thought the deeper view was an ". . . identity of European culture." The

Renaissance was a continuation of the earlier period, for the Middle Ages contributed directly to the revitalization of Hellenism: "By hastening the decline of art, by withdrawing interest from it and yet keeping unbroken the thread of its traditions, it has suffered the human mind to repose itself, that when day came it might awake, with eyes refreshed, to those ancient, ideal forms."[44] Though the direction of this age was negative, still it contributed to the renascence of spirit.

This is not to say that the Greek artistic ideal and Christian culture did not have oppositions. The spiritualist's interest grows as his conceptions are drained of the sensuous elements, while the senses are the very breath of the artist's life. The childlike and shameless vitality of the senses in Greek art was a delicate problem to Christian medieval art, which in a way tried to discredit the life of the senses; this was especially delicate because Christian art was dependent on pagan examples of artistic excellence. Moreover, Christian art had peculiar problems because of the very great difficulty of transforming Christianity into an artistic ideal. The Christian temper is full of the awareness of the transcendent God and His supernatural kingdom which, being essentially invisible, is very hard to express in art without drastic humanizing. One would think that the Incarnation provided the opportunity to show the Christian religion powerfully and beautifully in art forms, as indeed it has, for example, in the Byzantine tradition, but the human interest that is invested in such expressions has made Christian artists anxious about humanization. It could be argued that the Christian vision is unexpressible in its fullness. Pater judged, "Such forms of art, then, are inadequate to the matter they clothe; they remain ever below its level." He included Oriental art as well when he called such art ". . . over charged symbols, a means of hinting at an idea which art cannot fitly or completely express, which still remains in the world of shadows."[45]

But with the renascence of the Greek ideal, Christian art began to cope with its supersensible meaning by smiling in its tears. Renaissance artists began mixing pagan Humanism with Christianity, thereby giving forth a rich sensuous quality to their art. Da Vinci, whom Pater called the most profane of painters, and

Michelangelo, the master of pity, were the supreme results. The refulgence of human nature shone again even among the halos; Apollo and Christ reached out for each other in a blaze of beauty.

In his concluding essay on Winckelmann, Pater wrote:

> Certainly, for us of the modern world, with its conflicting claims, its entangled interests, distracted by so many sorrows, with many preoccupations, so bewildering an experience, the problem of unity with ourselves, in blitheness and repose, is far harder than it was for the Greek within the simple terms of antique life. Yet, not less than ever, the intellect demands completeness, centrality.[46]

Pater here testifies to a view of modern life which the existentialists have made dreadfully clear. And modern philosophers call out today for a completed intellect. This is to say, thinkers today would like to achieve some sort of intelligible compatibility between reason and religion so that modern man might achieve some unity with himself "in blitheness and repose." Pater perceived what Gabriel Marcel has called the stifling sadness of the contemporary world. Moreover, he realized that it made no sense to rebuke science or try to roll back the Industrial Revolution to try to reclaim some less weary past status. Far better possibility lay in marshalling other forces to counteract the dehumanizing effects of modernity. What Pater thought was needed was a special temper of mind which could cope with its existential condition with grace, power, and satisfaction. This is what he meant by "centrality." Where to get it but from religion and art. And when were the two last together in any sort of powerful union? In the Renaissance. There will be found examples of the kind of Humanistic temper which gives monumentality and meaning to human culture.

So Pater calls out for a rekindling of human powers along the lines of great achievements of past cultures. Though he was modernist enough to see the validity of extending certain scientific attitudes into the areas of the humanities and to be willing to look freshly at all tradition held near and dear, he still looked to the great Humanist minds to light new fires in his time. He judged, perhaps, that his times were becoming too centripetal, that is, that centers of powerful control were in formation which would stifle the human person. And thus he harkened back to the Greeks and their grand centrifugal culture in which, "Variety and novelty of experience, further quickened by a consciousness trained to an equally nimble power of movement, individualism, the capacities, the claim, of the individual, forced into their utmost play by a ready sense and dexterous appliance of the opportunity. . . ."[47] Here is what the modern world needed. So when Pater said to burn with a hard, gemlike flame, he meant something very old, very true, and very lost.

III

The juxtaposition of the minds of Hopkins and Pater would seem to suggest that, while they do have interesting points of resemblance, they really do not come together on the problems of modernity. Hopkins, for example, interested himself little with his times, apart from his literary and religious concerns. And Pater, once having dismissed religion and cleared away its repressions, bothered himself no more with it except for its aesthetic implications. These are, of course, stale cliches.

Despite the fact that Hopkins was deeply engrossed in his private religious and artistic problems, he lived in no monastery. From the time he was ordained, his ministerial service brought him into contact with the modern world. He served the Town and Gown at Oxford; he ministered the small industrial hamlet of Bedford Leigh near Manchester; he labored in a large parish church in the heart of a huge industrial complex—Liverpool; he taught in the political and social turmoil of Dublin. So Hopkins encountered the life of his times in rich and divergent ways and while he maintained a certain distance, he met and judged it with astonishing perception. The Industrial Revolution is a good instance. There is, for example, his famous declaration to Bridges of his sympathy with Communism for its just interest on the dreadful lot of the poor which he later memorialized in his "Tom's Garland." In explicating his declaration to Bridges, he emphasized its penetration in the reality of "the curse of our times."[48] Hopkins was deeply aware of a radical disorder in social order. He told Dixon, "My Liverpool and Glasgow experi-

ence laid upon my mind a conviction, a truly crushing conviction, of the misery of town life to the poor, of the misery of the
poor in general, of the degradation even of our race, of the
hollowness of this century's civilization: it made even life a
burden to me to have daily thrust upon me the things I saw."[49]

Moreover, Hopkins, sane English patriot that he was, could
not but see during his assignment in Ireland the faults of British
imperialism. Because he was Victorian and English he did not
disavow the Empire in theory, but he saw grave difficulties in
practice. These caused him to reconsider the Empire. He told
Patmore he could not but be critical of the Empire's mission to
bring freedom and civilization to other lands. This is not enough,
for freedom must be based on law though freedom alone must
bring the dissolution of the Empire: "No freedom you can give
us is equal to the freedom of letting us alone. . . ." As for bringing Christian civilization to the heathen, Hopkins asks what is
Christian about it? "But our Empire is less and less Christian
as it grows." This Hopkins tells Patmore as he praises him for
writing poems that are good deeds done for God and country.
Hopkins explains that fine works of art, works ideal in form
and high in matter, are a very great power in the world.[50] This
attitude is very much like Pater's Humanism, and it shows that
the larger implications of his own literary and religious trials
were not lost on him. The introduction of Christianity into his
own art and life is not unrelated to reintroducing Christianity
into Christendom.

Pater gradually and firmly disavowed a Humanism based on
human finitude and agnosticism. From the very beginning, he
saw the integral place of religion in culture, whether that of the
Renaissance or Greek. But in his early thinking, his mind was
on the aesthetic contributions of religion to culture, though in
his *Renaissance* with its aesthetic interests, there are genuine
counterbalances of authentic interest in the role of religion in
civilization. However, the most conclusive step was the writing
of *Marius The Epicurean*, for in this prodigious effort Pater had
decided that the Humanism he stood for needed a religious
phase and he here actively set out to explore a basis for religious
faith in his times.

As was his habit, Pater dealt with this modern problem (and his personal one as well) obliquely, through history and fiction. The obvious era to parallel with his own, considering that the issue was religious conversion, was roughly the period of catacomb Christianity. Happily there were intellectual and spiritual counterparts close enough to the nineteenth century to warrant this angle of approach.[51] However, the main value of this historical period was that it was an age of conversion. Men of all classes came to assent to the Christian faith in a milieu of immense profane distraction and mundane intellectuality.[52] What was their path of assent? Pater knew that religious commitment was intensely personal, and he was fully aware that the religious state arose from needs felt from the contact of real experience. So *Marius* is an autobiographical process which shows the development of the religious nature of man as he moves toward Christian conversion. Moreover, in keeping a constant movement towards Christianity, Pater still manages to lead the reader through a maze of philosophical considerations which, while they have relevance to the historical period, have far greater consequence to the Victorian crisis of belief.

Briefly, Pater traces the journey of a young man from his simple pagan piety through various states of hedonism and Stoic correctives to Christian belief. Pater portrays each phase openly and sympathetically and is careful to show that there is some truth in every phase which is worth carrying over to the next one. The result is a kind of organic spiritual development which makes the progress to Christianity have a coherent inevitability. The main point, which is made in each phase in ways that make up the drama in the book, is that a Humanism based solely on the human dimension, no matter how creative or subtle, does not satisfy the religious instinct of man. Pater exhibits this fault in the religion of Numa, Epicureanism, Cyrenaicism, and Stoicism. And the sediment of each in Marius only accentuates his real confrontation with doom, death, and decay—which each religion fails to meet satisfactorily. However Pater flirted with an agnostic and aesthetic Humanism in his *Renaissance*, in the decade that followed he firmly rejected this temptation and strongly espoused traditional Humanism with its theocentric base.

Moreover, a second critical fact is that in *Marius* Pater had concluded that no matter how creatively visionary the human mind could become, it did not have the power of transcendence. Some mediational power from Divinity had to come to the rescue of philosophy. Thus Pater accepts the idea of revelation which shows the way to Christ and the community He founded, the Church. The latter had always been immensely attractive to Pater in its liturgical life and in *Marius* he still exhibits a great predilection for the affective side of religion; but now this deeply emphatic effect of religion is even more intensified and surcharged, for it is now expressive of a passionate commitment born of a long spiritual quest and resting on a hard-won natural theology. It is Pater's insight about natural theology that I wish to stress. The parallel between the religious dilemmas of Marius and Pater is trenchant because in both the basis of religion is assumed to be some abstractive truths which would pass the rigors of a mathematical demonstration and then by some sort of assenting leap from this knowledge attain the heights of religious faith. Pater from the beginning in *Marius* is aware that religious faith is based on real knowledge and comes by way of an intuitive understanding which can never come from notional knowledge alone. Of course, Pater has Marius search through various philosophic systems in search for some answer because this was not only fictionally apt but also highly relevant to the positivistic approaches to religion of his time. To my mind, this is Pater's great development in *Marius*, for without it he could not have shown with any artistic conviction the absolute value of religion. And if his insight seemed ill-received and unheeded, he was in good company, for this is the principal awareness which Cardinal Newman made and on which he wrote his major work, and his eloquences have not fared much better.

There are those who do not see in *Marius* the jubilant espousal of the Christian faith, but rather a weak resignation on the doorstep of Christianity. Space does not permit a full documentation of Marius' assent to faith and the effects it had upon him. However, for those who ask some textual evidence for my reading, I would offer as highlights some of the following passages. The whole story of Marius underscores the discrediting of the absolute value of philosophy, the differences between the intuitive and abstractive, the real and the notional surfaces of awareness which are apparent at various times when Marius is probing a particular phase of his philosophic mind. Of course, the assent to faith is deeply personal and is often in close contact with concrete experience. Therefore, it is most difficult to exhibit artistically; even though the sights and shows are presented, the very mysterious internality of an act of faith makes any depiction of it highly ethereal, a quality that cannot be avoided. Still Pater is able to suggest some of the authentic qualities of religious assent. Here is an instance of Pater's awareness of the *locus* of faith:

But in the reception of metaphysical *formulae*, all depends, as regards their actual and ulterior result, on the preexistent qualities of that soil of human nature into which they fall—the company they find already present there, on their admission into the house of thought; there being at least so much truth as this involves the theological maxim, that the reception of this or that speculative conclusion, is really a matter of will.[53]

Pater unmistakably here states that religion rests on the rational powers of the will and not on those of the intellect, from which it follows that a metaphysical notion of God is an object of knowledge, not the personal God of religious worship. This is a fundamental distinction without which religious assent is dissolved inevitably in philosophic doubt, the very state of religion in Pater's time and, for that matter, in any time. Ultimately Hopkins was trying to uncover and maintain the same truth. Considering their very different predicaments, together they render an interesting judgment on Christianity in their times. If there was a meaningful and vital religious phase possible in modern times, this insight had to be recovered and freshly restated.[54] Like Kierkegaard, Hopkins and Pater saw that the renewal of Christianity was the main task of their time.

In consonance with assent in the real existential order, Pater,

in a long recapitulative chapter ("Second Thoughts"), has
Marius wondering about the possibility of a temporal order of
life in which reason and the will of God prevail, a divine order
". . . in the condition of human affairs—that unseen Celestial
City, Uranopolis, Calliopolis, *Urbs Beata*—in which a consciousness of the divine will being everywhere realized, there would
be, among other felicitous differences from this lower visible
world, no more quite hopeless death, of men, or children, or of
their affections."[55] Pater here indicates that religious faith cannot be an entirely personal experience, for it is by its very nature
social in that it is a personal encounter with a Presence whose
immensity is a total way of life. Yet Marius had discerned in his
friend Cornelius' Christianity that faith is intensely personal,
and that even though it is cut off from enactment in a benevolent
social order, its deep interiority seals it from hostile environ-
ments. Marius observes Cornelius during the crass brutality and
vulgarity of a circus: "Some inward standard Marius seemed
to detect there (though wholly unable to estimate its nature) of
distinction, selection, refusal, amid the various elements of the
fervid and corrupt life across which they were moving together:
—some secret, constraining motive, ever on the alert at eye and
ear, which carried him through Rome as a charm. . . ."[56] Here is a
solution to what Marius calls "a world's disillusion."

In a chapter called "The Will as Vision," Pater depicts Marius'
intuition of what Newman called "the unseen father." Marius asks
about ". . . an eternal friend to man, just hidden behind the veil
of a mechanical and material order, but only just behind it, ready
perhaps even to break through. . . ."[57] We are reminded of
Hopkins: "Since, tho' he is under the world's splendour and
wonder,/ His mystery must be instressed, stressed;/ For I greet
him the days I meet him, and bless when I understand."[58] Marius
wonders whether all he needs is to affirm this awareness: "Were
they doctrines one might take for granted, generously take for
granted, and led on by them, at first as but well-defined objects
of hope, come at last into the region of a corresponding certitude
of the intellect?"[59] This is a grammar of assent, the very phenomenology of which Newman put forth his greatest creative effort to
analyze. Pater, like Newman (unpublished papers indicate that

Pater was very interested in the *Grammar of Assent*), orders the process from the real to the notional, from religion to theology. When Marius asks, "Might the will itself be an organ of vision?"[60] he asks the very question to which Newman answers yes. He called it the "Illative Sense," and he meant by it an informal inferential process of reasoning upon real and concrete experience leading to a certitudinal assent. Upon this assent lie all acts of religion and notional assent to theological doctrines as well.[61]

The centrality of the Incarnation in Christianity is approached by Pater when he stresses Marius' need to share himself personally and intimately with what he calls "an impulse of lively gratitude." He had had earthly friends, but they simply accentuated his need for ". . . some other companion, an unfailing companion, ever at his side throughout; doubling his pleasure in the roses by the way, patient of his peevishness or depression, sympathetic above all with his grateful recognition, onward from his earliest days, of the fact that he was there at all? Must not the whole world around have faded away for him altogether, had he been left for one moment really alone in it?"[62] Hopkins put it: "No *better* serves me now, save *best*; no other/Save Christ: to Christ I look, on Christ I call."[63]

The salient passages of the coming of Marius' faith are too long to quote sequentially; Pater summarizes the growth of Marius' spirituality from intuition to conception:

Through one reflection upon another, he passed from such instinctive divinations, to the thoughts which give them logical consistency, formulating at last, as the necessary exponent of our own and the world's life, that reasonable Ideal, to which the Old Testament gives the name of *Creator*, which for the philosophers of Greece is the *Eternal Reason*, and in the New Testament the *Father of Men*— even as one builds up from an act and word and expression of the friend actually visible at one's side, an ideal of the spirit within him.[64]

The significance of this passage cannot be overstressed. It reveals how deeply aware Pater had become of the process of religious assent. He shows that assent begins with prime intuitions in the real order which lead to trust and affirmation, and that on this certitudinal basis, there is formulated "that reasonable Ideal" which he identifies as the very God named in Christian theology. Also, despite the conceptualization of God, Pater stresses the personal and concrete fundament of religious faith—"an act and word and expression of the friend actually visible at one's side. . . ." This is central to Hopkins' expression of faith: "—for Christ plays in ten thousand places,/Lovely in limbs, and lovely in eyes not his/To the Father through the features of men's faces."

Pater leaves little doubt that Marius experienced religious assent. He says that Marius felt some contact beyond himself and the material world:

. . . and he felt a quiet hope, a quiet joy dawning faintly, in the dawning of this doctrine upon him as a really credible opinion. It was like the break of day over some vast prospect with the "new city," as it were some celestial New Rome, in the midst of it. That divine companion figured no longer as but an occasional wayfarer beside him; but as an unfailing "assistant," without whose inspiration or concurrence he could not breathe or see, instrumenting his bodily senses, rounding, supporting his imperfect thoughts.[65]

There is a rush of charity in Marius' heart. He calls out prayerfully that his best moments and his sorrowful ones might be taken into an Eternal Consciousness: "Oh! that they might live before Thee."[66]

Pater also makes clear that this is no mere effusion of emotional yearning. He tells us that Marius is brought to an even more intense awareness of the spiritual quality of his life, of the need to recover a kind of radical innocence: "And again, the resulting sense of companionship, of a person beside him, evoked the faculty of conscience—of conscience, as of old and when he had been at his best, in the form, not of fear, nor of self-reproach even, but of a certain lively gratitude."[67] This is contrition out of love, the very heart of Christian penance. And Pater leaves no doubt that this is the most momentous event of Marius' life: "But for once to have come under the power of that peculiar mood, to have felt the train of reflections which belong to it really forcible and conclusive, to have been led by them to a conclusion, to have apprehended the *Great Ideal,*

so palpably that it defined personal gratitude and the sense of
a friendly hand laid upon him amid the shadows of the world,
left this one particular hour a marked point in life never to be
forgotten."[68] Newman, the master of the grammar of religious
assent, would have been gratified by Pater's depiction of the
coming of Marius' faith.

Pater had yet at this point in his book to specify Marius'
faith as Christian. This he sets Marius out to do immediately:
"Must not all that remained of life be but a search for the
equivalent of that Ideal, among so-called actual things—a gather-
ing together of every trace or token of it, which his actual
experience might present?"[69] Part Four of Volume II shows
Marius the identification of the Christian Church as the "equivalent of that Ideal." That Pater, after having drawn a picture of
the early Church which is immensely attractive to Marius and
which he begins to identify as God's vicar, has Marius die
before being formally received in the Church in a kind of cul-
minating triumph of faith. This has been taken by some readers
as a structural weakness which does damage to Pater's central
theme. Some have read this as Pater's inability to accept Christianity as the religion of his faith. R. V. Osbourn is correct, I
believe, in holding that Pater's fair presentation of the various
forms of life Marius considered before becoming a Christian has
misled many readers. He argues that Pater's artistic prudence
in handling his theme has, for anyone carefully following the
book's structure, enforced the culminative statement of the theme
that ". . . the life of the Christian community appears to be the
conclusive answer to the problems of the book's quest, a life
which is serene, social and complete, holding the 'prize of a
cheerful temper on a very candid survey of life.' "[70] He instances
the chapter "The Martyrs" as an example of Pater's deftness.
Marius dies a Christian through what theologians term "baptism
of desire." And Pater left no doubt about this. While dying in
the hut of some Christian peasants, his whole life crowding
before him, he perceives an image of Jesus. He dies with a
"sudden sense of peace and satisfaction,"[71] after being given
Holy Viaticum, anointed, and buried secretly (in their view) as
a martyr.[72]

It can be argued that Marius, even granting his Christian conversion, is a very long way from representing the kind of conversion open to a nineteenth-century Victorian. Of course, Marius' conversion does not solve either the Victorian or the modern religious dilemma. Indeed Pater recognized this, for it ought to be remembered that *Marius* was to be one of three works dealing with religion, the third one treating the end of the Enlightenment and presumably problems very apposite to the Victorian era. However, even though Pater never fulfilled his intention and thus has left us wondering, there is every reason to credit him, in *Marius*, with a primary insight, namely, that religious faith is grounded in the real knowledge of self-awareness. He is not alone in this, as I have suggested, but it is notable that a modern Humanist of his stature made such a radical correction of positivist Humanism. Pater thus anticipates the whole Existentialist movement in philosophy in its revolt against the philosophy of analysis and logicality. Marius saw into this long before Sartre or the "beat generation."

I do not wish to suggest that *Marius* presents conclusively Pater's solution to his own religious problems. I do believe that it is highly likely that *Marius* is a good facsimile of Pater's faith; I say this despite the report that Pater returned to the Church of England in his last years and died within its communion.[73] Trying to say something conclusive about Pater's Christianity is like trying to dispatch Hopkins' poetry. The most that can be said is that both seemed to have been placed on the doorstep of Divinity. If the destiny of Hopkins' poetry is any guide, we need not worry about the fate of Pater's soul.

Finally, I wish to re-emphasize my main contention. The genius of Hopkins and Pater come together in the affirmation of a single tradition of beauty and holiness. Each in his own way, through his own predicament, gave witness to this unicity as the truth of Humanism which is elemental to Western civilization and which, in their time, was in danger of being lost. Both sought a way to recover the real insights of natural theology through the creative powers of the imaginative reason, their own and those great ones of the past. Therefore, though Hopkins and Pater seemed to have taken quite opposite roads—Christianity and Hellenism—

they had to meet, if each pursued his path with integrity. As Werner Jaeger noted:

For whatever be the difference between Christian and ancient philosophy, they both agreed on the question which Aristotle raises at the beginning of his *Metaphysics* where he asks whether the idea of such a knowledge of the superhuman is not beyond human nature. Some of the old Greek poets seem to think so, he says, and they attribute that knowledge to God alone. But with his master Plato Aristotle refused to be a Greek in that sense and proclaimed an idea of man which includes the Divine and shows the way how mortal man may participate in eternal life.[74]

Sane beauty is immortal beauty: "God's better beauty, grace."

CHAPTER V

The Conscience of the Critic

I

ANY DISCUSSION of the critical philosophies of Pater and Hopkins ultimately revolves around the questions of the matter and the form of art. About the ends of art, Hopkins and Pater really had no quarrel. They both espoused a truly Humanistic goal of art —the soul of humanity and the glory of God. This may seem quite wrongheaded to those deceived by Pater's vacillatory blurring of Christianity and culture and Hopkins' Knights of Columbus demeanor about Christian commitment. Nevertheless, I think it is clear that Pater was no womb-to-tomb Humanist nor was Hopkins just a mission-brand Jesuit thumper. There is no doubt that Pater and Hopkins were in agreement about the service of art, perhaps most trenchantly stated by Hopkins: "What are works of art for? to educate, to be standards. Education is meant for the many, standards are for public use."[1] Pater put down the means: "Imitation:—it enters into the very fastnesses of character; and we, our souls, ourselves, are for ever imitating what we see and hear, the forms, the sounds which haunt our memories, our imagination."[2] That art plays an important part in shaping society neither denies; rather each asserts the very great responsibilities of the artist.

The discussion, then, lies in the fundamental question of the nature of art—the cunning juncture of its matter and form. Where Hopkins and Pater stood on this question and the large consequences of their stances is, in my opinion, an object lesson for modern criticism of the greatest import—one which I hope to make clear. Our age has been called a great age of criticism because of its depth and precision, hailed as greater than in any other critical writing done in the English language. I suggest that this praise needs a very large qualification.

First of all, let us see how Pater got himself into a critical quandary which anticipates and exemplifies the modern critical dilemma. In the Preface to his *Renaissance*, Pater laid down the aim of criticism as the discrimination of beauty in a work and the communicating of it to his readers.[3] To do this, Pater insisted that the critic not only must take into consideration his own sensibility, but also must make a careful estimate of the historic conditions in which the work was written as well as an attempt at defining the special temper of genius of the author who wrote in this milieu. This "historic sense" we have already seen in Pater's own philosophic and critical work.[4] Pater's idea of history was a "total history" in which a true sense of fact demanded a relativistic attitude towards any historical estimate, Pater especially emphasized this early in his career, perhaps never more extravagantly than in his essay on Coleridge. Pater saw the essential consideration of the critic's own sensibility as ". . . seeing one's object as it really is, is to know one's own impression as it really is, to discriminate it, to realise it distinctly."[5] So while criticism involved historicity and objectivity, these implied relativism and subjectivity, if, accordng to Pater, critical integrity is maintained.

An obvious question arises. If criticism means judgment according to standards, then how, in Pater's view of the critic's axioms, are standards to be derived? Pater, of course, saw the issue, and he answered that the element of permanence in the flow of history is the taste of genius whose standard transcends any age or culture.[6] We have seen that Pater looked to Greece for this standard which apparently he felt once and for all established artistic ideals. This is to say, Pater declared Hellenic artistry as critical orthodoxy and thus every succeeding age must have its culture judged by Grecian genius. What was the Greek genius? This is an historical question which, taking Pater's view of history, is not likely to be settled except relatively. Thus any derivable critical standards will necessarily be subjective. The result of this quandary was to make the very premises of criticism the first job of the critic. This is exactly what Pater did.

A central interest in Pater's *Renaissance* was to try to establish through the methodology he had laid down what the Hellenic artistic ideals were. Reading the Winckelmann essay as his distilled estimate of the essence of Greek art, we find Pater asking himself whether the culture which he has defined is now beyond human understanding and influence. Pater answers no. Winckelmann and Goethe penetrated into this antique world through passion and temperament.[7] They came to realize within themselves something of that ". . . balance, unity with one's self, consummate Greek modelling."[8] This is to say, they came to a deep and true awareness of the past in the present. What Pater was doing was confessing the genius of Winckelmann and Goethe as a kind of fresh surfacing of Hellenism. Attractive as Pater makes this, we are led from history, even relative history, to personality whose temper, however full of insight and however penetrating, still remains a puzzling subjectivity. From the thicket of history we go to the mews of personality, where we can find only aesthetic sense as a premise for critical judgment. This is the basic weakness of "The Conclusion," and apart from any other misleading aspects to which it was readily susceptible, this lack of critical principle was enough to make it worthwhile to reconsider it.

To define the critical conscience as basically aesthetic is to reduce critical judgment to impressionism. When one sorts through Pater's literary criticism, we do not find illuminating and specifying judgments; what we are given are richly suggestive, personal impressions. These pass for critical judgments even though these responses are wrought to a point of summary association of the work of art with the art of the critic. Pater, of course, is famous for this kind of criticism, for no one has excelled him in this impressionism. The result of this kind of

critical writing is another act of criticism, since what purported
to be the first act has become a work of art in its own right. This
is not to say that Pater exercises no critical function at all. He
does take us into an author through his own impressions; he
does try to light on the striking features of a work and convey
to us something of their significance. Perhaps Pater's strongest
point as a critic is his stress on the appreciatory attributes of an
author, attributes which he tries to share with his reader. Pater
does not analyze these qualities; he tries to exhibit relations
between the characteristics of the age and those of the work,
between the creative attributes of the author and the aesthetic
responses of his own sensibilities. The aim of the criticism is a
kind of empathic cohesion between work, author, age, and
response. Pater's criticism is syncretistic.

A survey of Pater's critical writing reveals that he attempted
two kinds of criticism—literary and philosophical. Taking up the
literary, we find a very uneven performance. In the essays on
Coleridge (the later version in *Appreciations*), Wordsworth,
and Thomas Browne, we are led into the minds and art of these
authors with a good deal of penetration and cognizance; however, there is no balance maintained between the work and the
artist (his public and private contexts). Pater seems always
more anxious to draw up the historical context and to fit the
author in, a critical skill he has not been praised enough for, perhaps because modern critics consider this an aside. Moreover,
Pater does point out what he considers to be flaws and defects
in the work of these authors: Coleridge's excess of seriousness,[9]
the duality of higher and lower work in Wordsworth,[10] the
desultoriness of Browne's manner.[11] Pater also exhibits courage
in his judgments, as when he affirms, contrary to current attitudes, Wordsworth's personal and poetic stature by arguing
that Wordsworth's isolation and detachment were means to
purify feeling.[12] Perhaps a more striking instance is Pater's essay
on Rossetti, in which he stands off contemporary charges against
Rossetti's work by admitting, somewhat diffidently, certain excesses in Rossetti but overshadowing these with what Pater considers the distinctive virtue of Rossetti's poetry, ". . . that sincerity of his, which allies itself readily to a serious beauty, a

sort of grandeur of literary workmanship, to a great style."[13]
The qualities of this style were "definiteness of sensible imagery,"
"imaginative vividness," "pictorial genius," harmony of matter
and form, and "transparency of language."

But even in these moments of critical strength, there is apparent
the besetting weakness of the aesthetic conscience, its inability
to find a rational equivalent for its artistic passion. Pater feels
deeply Rossetti's sincerity through the sensible immediacy of his
images, but he fails to perceive the intellectual vacuum that
pervades Rossetti's poetry, a vacuum which no amount of use
of conventional religious symbols dehydrated of their traditional
content can supply. Pater, it seems, mistook Rossetti's facility
with religious allusion as an enlargement of poetic sensibility
in his time, whereas it really marked a diminution, a befogging
disconnecting of mentality from sensibility.

Of course, it is this general satisfaction with pervasive feeling which is the greatest hazard for the aesthetic conscience.
Considering Pater's penchant for this sort of criticism, we are
pleased to discover the self-discipline with which he deports
himself generally. There are momentary lapses, such as when
he breaks out in his essay on Coleridge and speaks of the elusiveness of Coleridge's awareness: "What a distemper of the eye
of the mind! What an almost bodily distemper there is in
that!"[14] But seldom does Pater allow a critical performance to
be informed mainly by his good feelings as he does in his essay
on Lamb in which Pater's sensitivity for the pathetic in Lamb
makes his essay a caress rather than a criticism. In his essay,
"Shakespear's English Kings," a similar weakness for Richard II
is evident, though as R. V. Osbourn quite rightly points out,
Pater's approach to Shakespeare anticipates modern criticism
with his emphasis on the dramatic and poetic unity in the plays
he treats.[15]

This highlighting of Pater's criticism suggests that in the main,
Pater's conscience as a critic was aesthetic. It is fair to say that
Pater almost always took into consideration the historical contexts of the objects of his criticism, and while this afforded him
opportunities to make historico-aesthetic judgments, he was
never able to come to critical convictions based on what he

considered to be the truth of things as they stand. This is to say, his estimates of the significance of the matter of art, though meant to be philosophically full of insight, are most often vague and indeterminate. This is true even of his best efforts. Of Wordsworth whom he calls one of the masters in the "art of impassioned contemplation": "Their work is, not to teach lessons, or enforce rules, or even to stimulate us to noble ends; but to withdraw the thoughts for a little while from the mere machinery of life, to fix them, with appropriate emotions, on the spectacle of those great facts in man's existence which no machinery affects. . . ." Here he quotes, presumably Wordsworth, thus naming the categories of universal passions, interesting occupations, environment, accidents, discontent, sadness, and death.[16]

He says of Coleridge: ". . . his passion for the absolute, for something fixed where all is moving, his faintness, his broken memory, his intellectual disquiet, may still be ranked among the interpreters of one of the constituent elements of our life."[17] Or Rossetti: "For Rossetti, then, the great affections of persons to each other, swayed and determined, in the case of his highly pictorial genius, mainly by that so-called material loveliness, formed the great undeniable reality in things, the solid resisting substance, in a world where all beside might be but a shadow."[18]

What is meant by the "great facts"; "the constituent element"; "the great undeniable reality in things"? These are the weak expressions of an aesthetic conscience trying to say something judgmental about the matter of art. Pater's criticism constantly tries to creep up on a definitive idea, but we know that this will not happen because, as we have seen at length in his philosophic criticism, Pater's mind's eye was on the fluxing partiality of truth. It was the reality of the flicker and not the flicker of reality in thought that obsessed Pater. Therefore, when he as a critic tried to translate art into human values, he was left with aesthetic paradigms whose imitative transference into real life, he argues weakly in an unpublished essay on the aesthetic life, can take place in a kind of "osmotic" way. Pater put it in the "School of Giorgione," ". . . the meaning reaches us through ways not distinctly traceable by the understanding. . . ."[19]

There is no doubt in my mind that Pater saw this weakness in his critical work in general, for seldom does he fail to attempt some statement on the intellective value of the object of his criticism. If philosophical, then he seeks the perennial and universal strain in the thought; if literary, he tries to specify the mental temper of the author. All of which brings us to Pater's last great critical effort, a try at critical theory—his essay "Style." This is a very important essay in Pater's criticism and an even more important one as a presage of the direction of modern criticism. For in this essay, Pater meets head on the problem of the matter and form in literary art, perhaps the most formidable problem for the critic of aesthetic conscience. Pater first approached this issue in his essay, "School of Giorgione," in which he made the broad general statements from which his remarks in "Style" would come as deductions. Let us begin with the universals of his position.

Pater states as elemental this principle of the aesthetic critic: ". . . that the sensuous material of each art brings with it a special phase or quality of beauty, untranslatable into the forms of any other, an order of impressions distinct in kind. . . ."[20] Thus there are different kinds of aesthetic beauty, and it is the job of the critic to discriminate them. Yet, while this principle holds, there is a tendency of each art "to pass into the condition of some other art,"[21] and the direction of this movement is pure form:

All art constantly aspires towards the condition of music. For while in all other kinds of art it is possible to distinguish the matter from the form, and the understanding can always make this distinction, yet it is the constant effort of art to obliterate it. That the mere matter of a poem, for instance, its subject, namely, its given incidents or situation—that the mere matter of a picture, the actual circumstances of an event, the actual topography of a landscape—should be nothing without the form, this mode of handling, should become an end in itself, should penetrate every part of the matter: this is what all art constantly strives after, and achieves in different degrees.[22]

Pater goes on to note that while poetry "works with words addressed in the first instance to the pure intelligence; and it deals, most often, with a definite subject or situation,"[23] the ideal

types of poetry reduce the distinction between matter and form
to a minimum. Thus lyric poetry by this criterion is "the highest
and most complete form of poetry" whose perfection depends
upon "a certain suppression or vagueness of mere subject. . . ."[24]
According to Pater, "Art, then, is thus always striving to be
independent of the mere intelligence, to become a matter of
pure perception, to get rid of its responsibilities to its subject
or material. . . ."[25]

Why does the aesthetic critic have to obliterate an awareness
of matter in the form of art? The answer is obvious and Pater
knew it: the aesthetic critical conscience in itself has no criteria
by which to judge the import of the matter of art. It can answer
whether a given work is art, but to say how good, not to speak
of great, is truly beyond its capabilities, for in these questions
it must go beyond structure to matter, beyond feeling to mind.
Significantly, in his essay "Style" Pater tries to enlarge the scope
of the aesthetic critic beyond identifying a work as art. I am
suggesting that in this essay, Pater, fully committed to an historical sense of art and culture and yet completely convinced
of the primary worth of the aesthetic impact of art, tried to
reconcile this rift in his thinking. He tried to find a basis for the
aesthetic critic to go beyond identifying the singular beauty of
a work, and a clear sense of his own response to it, to some
judgmental estimation of its full, artistic worth.

Pater opens his essay by introducing the subject of the differences between prose and poetry. This brings him to announce
the formula of his essay: "the imaginative sense of fact." On
this basis, Pater enfranchises the artist in the world of factuality
while maintaining his distinct character. After pointing out that
all writers offer *their* sense of fact, Pater says of the imaginative
writer: "For just in proportion as the writer's aim, consciously
or unconsciously, comes to be the transcribing, not of the world,
not of mere fact, but of his sense of it, he becomes an artist, his
work *fine* art; and good art . . . in proportion to the truth of his
presentment of that sense; as in those humbler or plainer functions of literature also, truth—truth to bare fact, there—is the
essence of such artistic quality as they may have."[26] He concludes, ". . . all beauty is in the long run only *fineness* of

truth. . . ."[27] Moving to the literary artist, Pater ascribes to him a sense of "soul-fact," which is to say, ". . . of fact in its infinite variety, as modified by human preference in all its infinitely varied forms."[28] It follows, considering the enormity of fact in the modern world and its attendant naturalism, that the literary artist must be a scholar, must have the "scholarly conscience." Pater judged that only prose possesses the expressive capabilities to depict modernity, and he felt that scholarliness ought to make the literary artist even more scrupulous with language— "The right vocabulary!"[29]

The proper order of words which the literary artist constructs becomes for Pater the primary "fact" of literature: "By soul, he reaches us, somewhat capriciously perhaps, one and not another, through vagrant sympathy and a kind of immediate contact." This he distinguishes from mind in style, the "static and objective indications of design in his work . . . ," through which unity of design is achieved.[30] However, "soul" provides "unity of atmosphere . . . soul securing colour (or perfume, might we say?) as mind secures form, the latter being essentially finite, the former vague or infinite, as the influence of a living person is practically infinite."[31] "Mind" and "soul" come together in the crucible of the artist's imagination, and after long tempering, emerge as the intuitively known word—"the exact apprehension of what was *needed* to carry the meaning."[32] This is the birth of style whose "absolute accordance of expression to idea," according to Pater, is ineluctably "that finest and most intimate form of truth. . . ."[33] Because style is for the artist an "absolutely sincere apprehension of what is most real to him," while it represents a kind of self-revelation, it becomes through its imaginative fusion of matter and form impersonal, indeed becomes the primary fact of literature. So Pater concludes that ". . . literature, by finding its specific excellence in the absolute correspondence of the term to its import, will be but fulfilling the condition of all artistic quality in things everywhere, of all good art."[34]

Had Pater stopped here in his essay, I contend that he had not enlarged the judgmental scope of the conscience of the aesthetic critic. While I do believe that he gave a finer statement to the critical basis upon which aesthetic criticism operates, namely artistic structure, he did not find a way to avoid impressionism. Making structure a fact does not make aesthetic criticism objective, or provide it with standards, any more than the artist making his personal sense of fact into art provides him with the truth. Moreover, Pater's criterion of the exact correspondence of the word to the apprehension serves admirably as a norm of style, but it will not do for a definition of truth which needs something to be said about the quality of the apprehension in the first place. Pater's Coleridgean handling of the imaginative process misses that very quality which Pater did not like in Coleridge, "his passion for the absolute," without which he remains caught between the subjectivity of impressionism and the relativity of historicism. The same can be said of his philosophic criticism.

Pater allows himself as an aesthetic critic the judgment of whether a given work can be called good art, but I question that the aesthetic critic can even arrive at this. While there is no doubt that the expressive structure in all its wholeness is the proper focus of the critic, the formula to this artistic order, as Pater noted, was "the word's adjustment to its meaning," and consequently no complete criticism can be made which does not consider the intellectual status of the matter; indeed, no definitive aesthetic judgment can be rendered without weighing the import of the intellective (including intuitive) perspectives of the work under critical judgment. Pater's strong emphasis on the fusion of matter and form, following Coleridge, is well taken, especially at a time when new and more comprehensive concepts of history threatened to make works of art merely more data, and when naturalism and realism seemingly were theories of imaginative facticity. Clearly Pater was demarcating history and art in distinguishing "mere fact" from "a personal sense of fact." And while this distinction served to discipline the critic's sense of art by reminding him that the *locus* of criticism is the art object, imprudently applied, it could also reduce the proper critical interests which are mediated through artistic structure; for the great danger of structuralism is that in its heavy attention to artistic form, it reduces literature to a verbal formula.

Criticism then can only be either impressionistic or linguistic, depending on whether the structure is taken primarily as a highly organized stimulus or fact. Thus the initiatory question of criticism—Is it art?—becomes the only question; good or great art is a kind of judgment which exceeds the premise of structuralism because it opens up questions which go beyond artistic form to the mentality which that very form mediates.

Pater had the same trouble in his philosophic criticism. His stress on the mind as a limited factor in the attainment of truth served excellently to define the process of tradition so that it did not become petrifactive, yet the danger was that it would be misunderstood that partial truth was no truth at all. This is the weakness, to my mind, of Pater's study of Plato. Pater opened up the discursive implications of Platonic thought with insight and quite rightly stressed the transcendent, but suspended, visionary dimensions of Platonism. But in his zest for seeing the mental limitations accounted for in the Platonic temper, Pater unbalanced his view by not showing that Plato affirmed the mind's capacity for knowing the truth in a monumental way. One can read through *Plato and Platonism* and nearly forget that Plato was the greatest philosophical idealist in history. This disequilibrium arises from Pater's not being able to find a middle way between intellectual archaism, where tradition was stalled in his day and against which he was contending, and intellectual evolution in which tradition continues to develop and grow. History, including an estimate of the temper of genius, was the scholarly tool through which Pater saw the movement of culture, but he failed to see the developmental stages of the mind. Thus his historico-philosophic writings exhibit a certain inadvertence to the corrective process of the history of thought. While remembering that Pater was trying to recover a spirit he thought lost to his time, and hence his interests flow and change, still the stance of his thought strikes one as catatonic. It is as if he were frequently seized by the Hellenic spirit of judgment and truth, in all of its capacious grasp of reality, in his books and apparently in his conversation, only to fag before modern currents into pale assurances and the stupor of an agony made of a thousand little doubts. It is a fair criticism to say that Pater is his weakest in both mind and expression when confronting his own world. One feels a little gasp at these moments in Pater's books, as if his mental powers nearly stall before the steep inclines of his time. However, we must remember that Pater was searching for a true sense of tradition for his time which squared with historic tradition, an insight into the present of the surfacing past. For this we must honor him because he was searching for the great and true Humanism of Western culture during a time in which it seemed irretrievable. If he had not the mind to forge a new traditional synthesis, he had the insight of a need for one and the courage to begin a search. This is specially apparent in *Renaissance,* in *Marius,* in *Plato and Platonism,* and in his unpublished essays on the history of philosophy and moral philosophy.

A testament to the integrity of Pater's Humanism and to his awareness of the limitations of the conscience of the aesthetic critic is that he did not end his essay on "Style" on the limited, critical scope of impressionism. Rather, in a last paragraph which opened up to scrutiny the whole of his essay, he laid down the premise in which the act of criticism culminates and without which no criticism is complete. After allowing that the aesthetic critic can discern good art, he said: "Good art, but not necessarily great art; the distinction between great art and good art depending immediately, as regards literature at all events, not on its form, but on the matter."[35] Instancing Thackeray, he goes on: "It is on the quality of the matter it informs or controls, its compass, its variety, its alliance to great ends, or the depth of the note of revolt, or the largeness of hope in it, that the greatness of literary art depends, as *The Divine Comedy, Paradise Lost, Les Misérables, The English Bible,* are great art."[36] Here, I suggest, Pater does not contradict himself, nor does he abruptly dismiss aesthetic criticism as effete; rather he draws a careful distinction between one plane of critical response and another. He leaves no doubt which is the higher, and yet there is no reason to think that the higher vitiates the lower. What Pater makes quite clear is that the conscience of the critic is more than an aesthetic conscience, that no aesthetic criticism can pass for a complete critical act, for Pater is fully cognizant that the form of literary art is more than a complex verbal structure, that artistic form is the mediator of an apprehension of the real whose dimensions must count in the making of art as well as the judging of it. Thus Pater, in this last moment of his essay, provides a corrective on the aesthetic phase of criticism which serves to maintain the balance in criticism between the feeling and thought united in the mediative structure of art. Had Pater, of course, been more forthright in this matter earlier in his career, he could have avoided causing confusion between his aestheticism and decadence, an association for which there is no solid piece of evidence but that of logicality.

Modern criticism has been for some time obsessed with literary structure as a complex verbal fact to be analyzed. Gradually this analysis excepted all historical dimensions of literary art which were not linguistic, and thus in theory at least, reduced the critical act from the explication of meaning to decoding the verbal formula. This emphasis on linguistic facts tended to insulate the work from the incursions of higher critical quests. Moreover, the strong inhibition against asking any critical questions but those submissive to language analysis gives this criticism the appearance of taut objectivity and near mathematical conclusiveness. Of course, these "new critics" have not been content with the judgment that a work is art, for they constantly resort to their sensibilities in order to go on to the higher questions of good and great. Thus these critics are no less impressionistic than was Pater; the difference lies in the mode of their impressionism. Where Pater was overtly eclectic and rhetorically appreciative, the "new critics" have been laconically oracular with a kind of disembodied voice. Whether with a floating sigh or a calculated perplex, we still have but the initiatory act of criticism whose operative plane is aesthetic, and while it lays the basis for attempting the higher questions of meaning and significance by keeping us in contact with its sensible medium, it affords us no literary judgments other than the awareness of art as art.

Philip Appleman in an essay[37] on the split between the "scholars" and the "impressionists" in modern criticism offers

Pater as an earlier instance of this critical crisis. He particularly offers Pater's historical sense as a model to the new critics as a much needed corrective to their "subjectivity." While I agree that the new criticism could make much good use of "a sense of the past," I am not so sure that Pater's historicism offers any way out of impressionism. It did not for Pater, even though he was acutely aware of the need for getting beyond it and assiduously tried to use his historical sense to accomplish this. I said at the outset of this essay that there is an object lesson in Pater, but I did not mean Appleman's. I meant the one that Pater put in the last paragraph of his essay on "Style"—the quality of literary art depends "immediately . . . not on its form, but on the matter." The implication of this statement, it seems to me, is profound for criticism, for it affirms the proposition that the judgment of literary art is not solely aesthetic because the completeness of the critical act demands philosophical judgment. This is to say that the literary critic cannot fail to come to terms with meaning in art, and when he does, he has failed to come to the fullness of literary judgment. I quite agree with Appleman that this involves a sense of history. Still it demands more than this: it requires insight into the perennial philosophic spirit from which comes the standards of mind, its penetration and power, its grasp and gravity. While these need not be treated as absolutes, they are the highwater marks of human apprehension which cannot but be interfused with great art. In the unity of art, it is the critic's business to trace out the philosophic experience as well as the aesthetic.

Ultimately, then, what any criticism needs is a sense of reality, of things as they really are, or of getting as nearly as possible a deep hold of the best human insights into existence. This is another way of stating that what both the "scholars" and "new critics" need to regain is the spirit of Humanism in the wholeness of its traditional sense. The outstanding virtue of this Humanism is its unity of spirit and experience, its sense of a universal order of values out of which the greatest art has been produced and the greatest criticism written. It will take a considerable act of humility on the part of modern critics to admit that their dogmas must develop, that they must renew their minds along with their feelings, that the schizoid status of modern intellectuality is as much their problem as anybody else's, that criticism is a phase of a total human rationality, and that critics are first, last, and always men—these are the hard examens of the conscience of the critic. I admire Pater because I believe he tried hard to examine his conscience on some of these very difficult matters. We could do worse than emulate his temper of mind.

II

Donald Davie has called G. M. Hopkins the greatest critic of the Victorian Age after Arnold: "His opinions of the verse of his contemporaries chime almost exactly with the views reached, fifty years after his death, by the best modern poets and critics."[38] However, I suggest that it is not Hopkins' clairvoyance which ought to interest us most, but rather what was the makeup of the critical conscience which rendered the judgments which have stood up so well. It will be my main business here to typify Hopkins as a critic, though now and then I will juxtapose him with Pater and modern criticism.

At the outset, I see no reason for qualifying my judgment in reading Hopkins criticism that he was a Christian Romantic. In fact, there is more evidence to support this judgment. If we take "a sense of self" as the touchstone of Romanticism of whatever variety, it can be fairly said that no Romantic developed and refined this attribute as did Hopkins. Perhaps the most telling instance of this is Hopkins' notion of the artist. It is not surprising that in a long and elaborate dialectic on self that Hopkins came to see the artist as possessing a special virtue. This virtue was the ability to hold a special awareness of his own self "inscaping" the world, and in consequence, his art aimed at expressing this heightened distinctiveness. We have seen that the philosophic and theological implications of self and inscape have very profound and pervasive meanings for Hopkins. These must be taken into account in any experience of him or his work. Though it is the inscape of art I wish to highlight, it must be kept in mind that when Hopkins turned to literary criticism, he had a fully realized value system to power his judgments.

Thus when Hopkins looked to traditional literature for critical canons to employ in his comparative criticism, he sought writers whose works possessed striking instances of "selfbeing." This is to say that Hopkins took as his tests those writers who exhibited exceptional mental powers which art called into full action: ". . . . that the concentration, the intensity, which is called in by means of an artificial structure brings into play the resources of genius on the one hand, and on the other brings us to the end of what inferior minds have to give us. . . . Greatness is measured by the powerful action of mind under what we look on as difficulties."[39] For Hopkins, Milton was a supreme example of this greatness and became, for Hopkins' criticism, a touchstone: "His verse as one reads it seems something necessary and eternal. . . ."[40]

In literature, inscape of art involves style, and it was Milton's style which received Hopkins' special praise and study: "I have paid a good deal of attention to Milton's versification and collected his later rhythms. . . . I found his most advanced effects in *Paradise Regained* and, lyrically in the *Agonistes*."[41] It was Hopkins' judgment that Milton was one of the great English masters of style, by which Hopkins meant Milton had accomplished two things in his literary art: he had found a language fully responsive to his "selfbeing," and, at the same time, a way of using language in a counterpointing structure which gave, Hopkins believed, the communicative verve of current speech while still retaining its elevated, poetic character. Hopkins told Dixon that he found his sprung rhythm in Milton's counterpoint, though it is not my purpose to go into this here.[42] What I wish to stress is that this distinctiveness of style unites with inscape of self through the powerful fusions of the imaginative intellect to become an artistic utterance of ". . . the very make and species of man as created both in him and in all men generally."[43] It was this white-hot fusion of the "selving" word in the fullness of poetic passion which struck Hopkins so forcibly as the highest kind of literary art. We are reminded of Pater: ". . . 'The style is the man,' complex or simple, in his individuality, his plenary sense of what he really has to say, his sense of the world; all cautions regarding style arising out of so many natural scruples as to the medium through which alone he can expose that inward sense of things, the purity of this medium, its laws or tricks of refraction. . . . Style in all its varieties, reserved or opulent, terse, abundant, musical, stimulant, academic, so long as each is really characteristic or expressive. . . ."[44] While both Pater and Hopkins assert that the highest artistic utterance takes on the impersonality of the universal, their understanding of the relation of art and personality is one we have come to characterize as Romantic.

It was not only counterpoint Hopkins found in Milton. There were other qualities that go into greatness of style. Currency of language meant a plague on archaism, and to say this meant to condemn a great deal of Victorian poetry. There are no more incisive remarks in the whole of Hopkins' criticism than those about literature written in a dead style, and he is even unstinting with the work of his literary correspondents, Bridges, Patmore, and Dixon. Time and again he attacks this failure in their works. Two instances will have to serve as examples. One is regarding the style of Canon Dixon. Hopkins allowed that Dixon employed sometimes an archaic style with a certain mastery, but ". . . still I cannot think even so it is right: I look on the whole genus as vicious."[45] The other example is a little sardonic. When Bridges remarked that Doughty's style was purer than Victorian English, Hopkins replied:

You say it is free from the taint of Victorian English? H'm. Is it free from the taint of Elizabethen English? Does it not stink of that? for the sweetest flesh turns to corruption. Is not Elizabethan English a corpse these centuries? No one admires, regrets, despairs over the death of the style, the living masculine native rhetoric of that age, more than I do; but " 'tis gone, 'tis gone, 'tis gone." He writes in it, I understand, because it is manly. At any rate affectation is not manly and to write in an obsolete style is affectation.[46]

Now it was Hopkins' judgment that ". . . a perfect style must be of its age," and that Milton's was a perfect style. Hopkins believed that Milton marked the highest point of development

of English style, which is to say that in Milton English attained
its best balance of currency and elevation. Moreover, Hopkins
thought the first generation of Romantic poets attempted to
perpetuate this standard of English, and though they were not
as forthright as Hopkins would have liked, nevertheless, their
poetic diction and style were in the tradition of the true standard. Hopkins noted this in a letter to Dixon in which he reviews the whole of contemporary poetry: "The Lake poets and
all that school represent, as it seems to me, the mean or
standard of English style and diction, which culminated in
Milton but was never very continuous or vigorously transmitted,
and in fact none of these men unless perhaps Landor were
great masters of style, though their diction is generally pure,
lucid, and unarchaic."[47] Added to these last mentioned qualities, Hopkins also found in Milton what he called "sequence of
phrase," which Dixon elaborated upon: "There is in Milton, as
I think a sort of absolute precision of language which belongs
to no other poet: a deliberate unrolling as if of some vast material, which is all there already, and to which the accident of
the moment in the writing can add nothing: a material which
his mighty hands alone can grasp, unroll, and display."[48] Hopkins also mentioned a second quality, "sequence of feeling,"
(which Dixon judged was less in Milton than in some other
writers) by which Hopkins meant ". . . a dramatic quality by
which what goes before seems to necessitate and beget what
comes after, at least after you have heard it it does. . . ."[49]

Hopkins' preoccupation with making poetry out of the living
speech of the day coincides with this distinctive Romantic trait
of Wordsworth and Coleridge, for these writers perceived that
something had gone false in the poetic diction of their time.
Each was searching for fresh ways to make poetry regain its
old passion and power. Wordsworth looked for it in the back-
waters of life, as if the language men really speak with any
primal qualities was more likely spoken under a tree than a
lamplight, but this was more the temper of Wordsworth than
Rousseau's regressive theory of history. The important difference between Hopkins and Wordsworth lay in their attitudes
towards the making of poetic language in the first place. Words-

worth understood it as something innate which the proper rec-
ollection would bring out, while Hopkins considered it to be
something deliberately made out of the complex of the history
of language. Thus Hopkins thought that poets could best be
classified by what he called their "keepings," by which he meant
the quality of historic sense of the literary mind palpably employed in the making of literary art.[50] For instance, he judged
that Keats and his imitators chose medieval keepings strongly
colored by the Elizabethan age. What impressed him about
Milton, then, was that his style had been made of a potently expressive amalgam of his own diction and a compound of English idiom partly from currency and partly from the tradition
of literary artifice up to that time, and all of this forged together
with deliberate mastery. This shows Hopkins to be much closer
to Coleridge's views of art and language, though not opposed
to the spirit of Wordsworth.

We have already seen Pater's great concern for the artifice
of the word in his essay on style. I judge Pater much closer to
Wordsworth than Hopkins, for the major stress seems to be the
intuition of style. For Pater, Flaubert was the "saint of style,"
and he described the process in what I would dub the Words-
worthian mode: "Coming slowly or quickly, when it comes, as
it came with so much labour of mind, but also with so much
lustre, to Gustave Flaubert, this discovery of the word will be,
like all artistic success and felicity, incapable of strict analysis:
effect of an intuitive condition of mind, it must be recognized
by like intuition on the part of the reader, and a sort of immediate sense."[51] However, we must remember that Hopkins, in
his famous categorization of the languages of poetry, left room
for such a language and style.[52] Moreover, Pater, in common
with the first Romantics and Hopkins, expressed in his usual
oblique way an interest in renewing literary language. In a
chapter titled, "Euphuism," in *Marius*, Pater involves his main
character in the literary endeavor of "the rehabilitation of the
mother-tongue, then fallen so tarnish and languid. . . . The
popular speech was gradually departing from the form and rule
of literary language, a language always and increasingly artificial."[53] Later Pater writes of a literary program as "partly con-

servative or reactionary, in its dealing with the instrument of the literary art; partly popular and revolutionary, asserting, so to term them, the rights of the *proletariate* of speech."[54] Even later, he talks about the theory of Euphuism in every age as being the awakening of literary conscience towards language and expression.[55] While this is generally true, this awakening was especially weighty on the Romantic literary conscience.

Moreover, I suggest that Hopkins' emphasis on the deliberate forging of a style is an element of subjectivity in the process of literature which goes towards distinguishing one poem from another, one poet from another, one age from another. Of course, Hopkins' strong concern for distinctiveness in style is a Romantic quality, but only in degree, for there is a kind of perennial Romanticism in every literary age wherein work is done which takes on the distinctive qualities of its time, its creator, and the whole of literary tradition. This mastery, as Hopkins understood it, was not the dominance of the personality of the artist over the creation, a kind of Romantic decadence of which Donald Davie accuses Hopkins, but rather a powerful execution of artistic power through which speech is framed for contemplation, as Hopkins put it, and added: "Some matter and meaning is essential to it but only as an element necessary to support and employ the shape which is contemplated for its own sake."[56] Like Pater, Hopkins understood that the "shape" takes on a certain impersonality in its made state. He criticized the lyric poetry of Dixon as being ". . . without centrality or reference to one point."[57] In his judgment of drama, Hopkins discourses on the "unities" marking the importance of unifying order.[58] And we have seen in his "sequence of phrase" and "sequence of feeling" how he insisted on what he called "connectedness." Hopkins says of contemplation (by which he means both reasoning and also a kind of intensely joyful dwelling upon) and structure: "Art exacts this energy of contemplation . . . for full enjoyment, the synthesis of the succession should give, unlock, the contemplative enjoyment of the unity of the whole."[59] Hopkins explained the principle of verbal order that goes to make up the artistic unity fit for contemplation in the following way. Words (thing-words) have three terms: prepossession of feeling (its connotative powers), its definition (including its phonology), and its extension to other things. What Pater called "*mind* in style," that is, the architectural conception of the work, is put by Hopkins this way:

The further anything, as of a work of art, the organisation is carried out, the deeper the form penetrates, the prepossession flushes the matter, the more effort will be required in apprehension, the more power of comparison, the more capacity for receiving that synthesis of (either successive or spatially distinct) impressions which gives us the unity with the preposession conveyed by it.[60]

This is Hopkins' sense of organic form in poetry, a notion which Herbert Read considers elemental to Romanticism and in England best expressed by Coleridge. Hopkins' stress on "synthesis" is akin to Coleridge's idea of "esemplastic" fusion in which a host of opposites in the conscious and the unconscious are reconciled in the impersonalizing order of the expressive structure of art. And like Coleridge, Hopkins understands this imaginative power as basically intuitive though in the fullness of and wholeness of its expression, there is a deliberating making-mastery.

It is important to note that Hopkins said "speech framed for contemplation," which brings up his attitude toward heightening speech—rhetoric. Hopkins judged the lack of rhetoric as "the universal fault of our literature. . . ." He went on: "By rhetoric I mean all the common and teachable element in literature, what grammar is to speech, what thoroughbass is to music, what theatrical experience gives to playwrights." The basic motive of rhetoric was what Hopkins called "bidding," by which he meant ". . . the art or virtue of saying everything right *to* or *at* the hearer, interesting him, holding him in the attitude of correspondent or addressed or at least concerned, making it everywhere an act of intercourse—and of discarding everything that does not bid, does not tell."[61] Twentieth-century critics generally agree with Hopkins that his whole century's literature lacked an effective sense of rhetoric and nowhere more defectively than in drama. Of course, it was bidding that Hopkins aimed at as a writer, which explains what he meant when he

said his poetry should be read by the ears, for many of the odd-
ments of his style are rhetorically directed effects of bidding.
What interests us here, however, is that bidding suggests the
distinctive voice of the poet addressing us, and since Hopkins
associates it with the Classical ideals of style, we must look
into the relation between bidding-speech and inscape.

We have seen already the general philosophical implications
of inscape and their kinship with the Romantic sense of self.
Now we must consider what the further implications are of the
inscape of speech [the style as man in Pater's essay] and inscape
itself. It is important to realize that there are two applications
of inscape which Hopkins makes to art. One has to do with the
writer's expressive forms, and one has to do with his insight
into existence. It is the artistic wedding of the two which gives
the shape to the work of art which is fit for contemplation. Up
until now our attention has been primarily directed towards the
inscape of speech, that is, style and all of its craft. These, as
Hopkins noted, were learnable and thus come under the critic's
judgment immediately. Thus Hopkins' letters to his literary
friends are filled with sharp lessons of failure in craftsmanship.
However, there are other qualities which inscape of speech
must possess besides currency, clarity, and elevation. These
must add up to what Hopkins called "a mounmental style" to
be truly classical, a style he attributed to the Greeks and to
Shakespeare. This is to say that a monumental style possesses
what Hopkins called "a mastery of execution": "Now this is
the artist's most essential quality, masterly execution: it is a
kind of male gift and especially marks off men from women,
the begetting one's thoughts on paper, on verse, on whatever
the matter is; the life must be conveyed into the work and be
displayed there, not suggested as having been in the artist's
mind. . . ."[62] Thus it is clear that inscape of speech does reveal
the inscape of the artist's person, the range and grasp, the passion and the power. This is what Hopkins admired in Milton's
artistic self, and so did Dixon, who called it "self-sufficiency,"
the personal power to "grasp, unroll, and display."[63] It follows,
then, that the work of art is an emblem of the artist in a profound sense.

It is significant that this sort of identity of the artist and art has been seen as the "general basis of the Romantic Movement in Europe," for, as Herbert Read puts it, "the romantic principle asserts that form is an organic event, proceeding from the intiutive experience of the artist. . . . Form belongs to the realm of essence and is abstracted from it by the mediating genius of the artist—genius, in this sense, being not the artist himself, but an unconscious power which he possesses (or which possesses him) and which enables him for a moment to identify himself with the formative energy of the universe, with *natura naturans.*"[64] Read has put together under *form* what Hopkins distinguishes as inscape of speech and inscape of existence, but there is no doubt that what Read calls organic form, and Hopkins synthesis, mean the same thing. Thus inscape of speech is not "self-regarding ingenuity" as Donald Davie would have it,[65] but truly human utterance: "A true humanity of spirit, neither mawkish on the one hand nor blustering on the other, is the most precious of all qualities in style. . . . After all it is the breadth of his human nature that we admire in Shakespeare."[66] And as Dixon said of Hopkins' master of the monumental style, Milton: "His matter is more external to himself than in other poets: and at the same time he and his poem make one whole, so that when you think of the one (I mean when you are not reading him) you think of the other also: when you think of the poet, you think of him in relation to his poem."[67] This is the impact of a truly distinctive inscape of speech.

To assert that Hopkins was possessed of a Romantic critical conscience is not to put him down as merely impressionistic, any more than showing Hopkins' Romantic cast of mind makes him a relativist. Herbert Read lays down for all genuine Romanticism what I have insisted on for "pure" Romanticism—that the basis of the Romantic movement was a recovery of a philosophical insight long and fruitfully held in Western Humanism, or as he put it, "The form is realized by the artist in the act of intuition: in the moment of his penetration of the veil of appearances that separates man from the real of essence."[68] And

we have already seen that Pater also uses the moment of intuition as a key to style and the man. According to this brand
of Romanticism, then, the element of subjectivity is a powerful
factor in the shaping of art, indeed one of its primary distinc-
tions. However, the very creative act of the artist necessarily
involves the philosophic mind of the artist and thus the shape
of his work, its very organic unity, confronts us with a complex
structure whose contemplation leads us into reality as the mind
expressively grasps it. The implications of this are great for the
critical conscience, for if this is the true nature of artistic structure, then the hierarchy of critical questions I have argued for
is established. This is to say that the aesthetic question is the
lead-off question which can only be conclusively answered by
judging the quality of humanity in the total work. Only then
can we have a complete criticism as well as a judgmental criticism. And this priority of critical order following the creative
order was maintained by Hopkins just as firmly as by Coleridge:
"Poetry is in fact speech only employed to carry the inscape
of speech for the inscape's sake—and therefore the inscape must
be dwelt on."[69] That is, the "inscape of speech" carries the "inscape of being," and hence poetic structures are made up of
repetitive parallelisms[70] which cast forth the poet and reality
in analogical word structures which, for the artistic moment,
are united in the harmonious order of the poem. Of course, the
critic's eye is constantly on the poetic form which mediates the
philosophic insight. In and through and by inscape of speech
we reach inscape of self and selves.

Hopkins insists upon philosophical principles as a requisite of the greatest art. Like Arnold, he laid down his own notion of "high seriousness": "This leads me to say that a kind
of touchstone of the highest or most living art is seriousness; not
gravity but the being in earnest with your subject—reality."[71]
This is the other side of Hopkins' criticism. Along with a patient and detailed examination of the technical matters of the
poetry of his friends, Hopkins disallowed any philosophical
frivolity. For instance, knowing Dixon's Christian commitment,
he came down hard on the heathen spirit in a poem purporting

to be a serious treatment of a subject central to his "principles."[72]
And there are other examples where he chides Dixon for play-
ing his "seriousness" falsely.[73] Perhaps a key example of Hopkins' application of "being in earnest" was his attitude toward
mythology, for in his judgment of a poet's use of myth we see
the critical prudence with which he sought to employ the philosophic principle in art. In a magnificent letter to Dixon, Hopkins explained his attitude towards Greek mythology. At the
outset he praised its beauty and excellence: "It is free from that
cumber of meaningless and childish rubbish which interrupts
and annoys one even in the midst of fine invention in for instance the Irish legends."[74] However, historically this mythology was religion and thus to a Christian, heathenism. Hopkins
could not see how any writer could take the Greek gods seriously without blemishing his efforts in a preposterous way. This
is precisely the criticism he made of Bridges' *Ulysses*. Bridges
took Athene seriously in his play and thus asked his reader to
do so: "Bridges took her almost seriously: so then did I, and was
disgusted. But I hold it was a false step of his: the heathen gods
cannot be taken seriously on our stage; nowadays they cannot
even be taken humourously. . . ."[75] Looked at as religion, Greek
mythology was not only untrue, according to Hopkins; it was
also sacrilegious:

For myself literally words would fail me to express the loathing and
horror with which I think of it and of man setting up the work of
his own hands, of that hand within the mind the imagination, for
God Almighty who made heaven and earth. Still he might set up
things perfect in their kind. But the Greek gods are rakes, and unnatural rakes. Put that aside too; put yourself in the position of a man
who like Homer first believes in them, next forgets or passes over
their wickedness: even so are the Greek gods majestic, awe inspiring,
as Homer that great Greek genius represents them? They are not. The
Indian gods are imposing, the Greek are not. Indeed they are not
brave, not self controlled, they have no manners, they are not gen-
tlemen and ladies. They clout one another's ears and blubber and
bellow. You will say this is Homer's fun, like the miracle-plays of
Christendom. Then where is his earnest about them? At their best
they remind me of some company of beaux and fashionable world
at Bath in its palmy days or Tunbridge Wells or what not.[76]

Now some modernists will smile and say that Hopkins had little understanding of the anthoropological import of myth, not to speak of its psychological side, and that he has let his Christian faith bias him unduly. However, while it can be readily conceded that Hopkins' understanding of myth did not come up to modern awarenesses, nevertheless this is beside the point, for the issue is basically whether a contemporary writer can take Greek mythology seriously in his art and still be in earnest with reality. Can he employ it in any way other than an expressive mode, be he Christian or almost any sort of modernist? The answer is surely no, if he wishes to give his work any quality of seriousness, much less "high seriousness." The same is true for the critic whose seriousness must equal the height of the artist's.

Of course, Hopkins both as author and critic believed that myth could be used to great advantage in literature, even in works of the highest earnestness, as he told Dixon: "But I grant that the Greek mythology is very susceptible of fine treatment, allegorical treatment for instance, and so treated gives rise to the most beautiful results. No wonder: the moral evil is got rid of and the pure art, morally neutral and artistically so rich, remains and can be even turned to moral uses."[77] So it is a question of artistic prudence in the light of the earnestness of his genuine intuitions into the real. Of course, if an artist or critic maintains merely an historical or relativist perspective in these matters, then he cannot and will not confront the full implications of the structural synthesis of art, and he will be left to play word games or sort out historical curiosities, or psychoanalyze the author. There is a question whether any of this is any more critically relevant than Pater's rhapsodizing his personal appreciations. Any of this can take on significance, surely, insofar as it leads to the higher critical questions.

There is in this same letter to Dixon a telling example of Hopkins' critical mind on the whole question of the matter of literature. The author in question is Wordsworth and Wordsworthians, among whom Dixon could not count himself. Hopkins replied, ". . . here, my dear friend, I must earnestly remonstrate with you; must have it out with you."[78] Hopkins goes on to write a ringing judgment and appreciation (one which ought to be set against some of Pater's for its piquancy) of Wordsworth's great ode, *Intimations*. The judgment I wish to cull out for our attention here is on the import of the matter of the poem; after noting that Wordsworth was an imperfect artist, Hopkins lays down his critical prinicple upon which he judges Wordsworth: ". . . as his matter varied in importance as he varied in insight (for he had a profound insight of some things and little of others) so does the value of his work vary. Now the interest and importance of the matter were here of the highest, his insight was at its very deepest, and hence to my mind the extreme value of the poem."[79] He goes on to say before pointing out some of the excellencies of rhyme, rhythms, diction, and feeling in the ode: "His powers rose, I hold, with the subject: the execution is so fine."[80] There is little doubt that Hopkins agreed with Pater that great literature depends immediately on the matter, and it is clear that the artistic consequences bear very heavily on the gravity of the matter. Hopkins said as much in an axiomatic statement which, in my opinion, accounts for the variation of tastes in terms of the synthesis of words and content. He noted that the contemplation which art energizes is more sane when the contemplation is of "that which really is expressed in the object," and less sane when the contemplation received is by way of "the least organic, expressive, by the most suggestive, way." This is to say that in the first contemplation the form of art is kept constantly in attendant mediation, while in the second the form is separated. As Hopkins said, "the prepossession and the definition, uttering, are distinguished and unwound. . . ." Out of this difference come preferences for "very sharp and pure dialectic" or "hard and telling art-forms." But whichever, in them we have "the two axes on which rhetoric turns."[81] That is, the temper of mind of the artist which calls forth the bidding-word, the rhetorical motive, the synthesis of which lays itself open more to one kind of contemplation than to another, and it is here that the examination of the critical conscience begins.

A sampling, or even an estimate, of Hopkins' critical performance need not be made here. W. H. Gardner has given us a careful sorting of Hopkins's critical judgments as well as a sound estimate.[82] And there have been others.[83] What I should like to highlight is Hopkins' notion of the true critic. Unlike many other poets, Hopkins did not disdain the critic. He said very early in his career: "Criticism is a rare gift, poetical criticism at all events, but it does exist," and this was said in a letter in which he defended criticism and critics "of genius, of deep insight, of great delicacy, of power, of poetry, of ingenuity, of everything a critic should have."[84] After pointing out how he was disgusted by bad criticism, he again noted, "A perfect critic is very rare, I know." Contrary to those who might have expected in a man so single-minded very little critical generosity, there was in Hopkins a conviction about this gravest defect in critics: "The most inveterate fault of critics is the tendency to cramp and hedge in by rules the free movements of genius, so that I should say, according to the Demosthenic and Catonic expression, the first requisite for a critic is liberality, and the second liberality, and the third, liberality."[85] Of course liberality is a giving and taking through what Hopkins called, in a letter to Bridges near the end of his life, "a passion for explanation." He added, "we should explain things, plainly state them, clear them up, explain them; explanation—except personal—is always pure good; without explanation people go on misunderstanding; being once explained they thenceforward understand things; therefore always explain: but I have a passion for explanation and you have not."[86] It would be hard to give a better description of the character of Hopkins' own criticism.

It is not entirely fair to set Hopkins against Pater as critics because there is a question as to whether Pater qualifies as a critic in the fullest sense at all. I do not wish to demean Pater's critical achievements; indeed, they have received far less estimation than their true worth. Still, there is a very great difference between a passion for appreciation and one for explanation. As Graham Hough noted, Pater's criticism is "the triumph not of a purpose but of a temperament."[87] Moreover, no critic can be fully evaluated on the basis of his judgments alone. There is the question of his prose. And here again, the stylistic prac-

tices of Hopkins and Pater are strikingly different. This difference was perhaps best put by Hopkins in a letter to Coventry
Patmore in which he tells Patmore what is wrong with his (and
Cardinal Newman's!) prose: "Each thought is told off singly
and there follows a pause and this breaks the continuity, the
contentio, the strain of address, which writing should usually
have."[89] Later he says of Newman: "His tradition is that of cul-
tured, the most highly educated conversation; it is the best
flower of Oxford life." Pater's style, I submit, is a version of
this, admirably suited for impressionism perhaps, but hardly
the manner of critical vigilance. As for Hopkins' style, what he
said of Dryden, I believe, applies to his own style as he said
it did: "What is there in Dryden? Much, but above all this: he
is the most masculine of our poets; his style and his rhythms
lay the strongest stress of all our literature on the naked thew
and sinew of the English language. . . ."[89] This is the style of
executive judgment whose great prowess is sustained and meticulous attention, and whose effect upon the mind is indelible.

Josephine Miles has shown how Hopkins' descriptive language is in the tradition of Keats as well as Milton,[90] and Dr.
Gardner has suggested that Hopkins' sense of self bears heavy
resemblance to the Romantics. I have here tried to show that
his critical conscience was formed on those principles of the
Humanistic tradition which in the nineteenth century went by
the name of Romanticism. Moreover, if there is a lesson for
modern critics in Pater, surely there is one in Hopkins. That lesson is the absolute necessity of the critical conscience to be
formed on philosophic as well as aesthetic principles, for after
all there is no escape from either historicism or impressionism
except in the integrated mind. I am not saying that criticism of
any whole value can only come from a mind committed to the
same perspectives as Hopkins; I am saying that it has only
come from minds integrated like his. Or as Graham Hough
puts it: ". . . it is just to say that the most vigorous and decisive
criticism, in any of the arts, has been done either in the service
of recognized tradition, like that of Johnson or Sir Joshua Reyn-
olds; or as jungle-clearing for contemporary creative work, like
that of Dryden, Coleridge, or, in our own day, T. S. Eliot and

Roger Fry."[91] And I am saying that much of modern criticism is a half-criticism, excellent as some of it is, or at least not a complete performance. This has justly been viewed as a crisis because, as Hopkins said about a reputation for judgment, "nothing so impairs that reputation as the strong assertion of half-truths."[92] And is not criticism in essence a reputation for judgment?

The Handsome Heart

IT WOULD BE QUITE EASY to draw up a summary of the many cross-patterns of the lives of Pater and Hopkins, because as men they were so much alike and because they cared about so many of the same things. However, pointing out that they both burned their poetry, for instance, has just as much significance in itself as the last enigmatic entry in an appendix of Thomas Wright's biography of Pater: "Pater calls St. Ignatius Loyola, 'the purest of saints.'"[1] The clusters of affinities give us questions, but no answers. Of course, there are questions which we can begin to answer. One, to my mind, fundamental question should be asked here: Is there a basic pattern out of which come the deeply held convictions of Hopkins and Pater?

In my judgment there is a profoundly personal commitment common to Pater and Hopkins, and this is the harmony of the beautiful and the good. It is true that this harmony is not easily maintained and surely is most difficult to achieve. Nevertheless, in both of these men there was a lifelong dedication to the good and the beautiful as they appear in life and are expressed in art. Both Hopkins and Pater looked to life as the inspiration of art, and to art to become a consequence in life. In so doing, each of them discerns in beauty an ethical contingency as a necessary condition to the fullness of the beautiful. This is to say that when beauty and good are properly unified (in life or in art), there is true holiness. There will be those who will chafe at such an assertion, but, as Graham Hough noted, ". . . one who has never known the beauty of holiness is not likely to know very much, in the end, about either holiness or beauty."[2]

True holiness threads the thinking and writing of Hopkins and Pater almost everywhere. It was in Pater's mind in the last essay in his last published book, virtually on its last pages: "And Platonic aesthetics, remember! as such, are ever in close connexion with Plato's ethics. It is life itself, action and character, he proposes to colour; to get something of that irrepressible conscience of art, that spirit of control, into the general course of life, above all into its energetic or impassioned acts."[3] In Hopkins, if anything this subject is a perennial topic, though perhaps he never put it more effectively than in a letter to Bridges: "I think then no one can admire beauty of the body more than I do, and it is of course a comfort to find beauty in a friend or a friend in beauty. But this kind of beauty is dangerous. Then comes the beauty of the mind, such as genius, and this is greater than the beauty of the body and not to call dangerous. And more beautiful than the beauty of the mind is beauty of character, the 'handsome heart.'"[4] This is as Plato would have it, certainly Pater, and what I have argued for in literary judgment: artistic genius informed by character.

In some sense, then, the achievement of true holiness is the story of Hopkins and Pater. Of course, each approached it his own way and tried to realize it according to his own capacities. Moreover, it is true that Pater had the beautiful as his leading aspiration as Hopkins had the good; however, these were but the advance elements of their deeper intentions. I believe any student of the two should be wary of separating too widely either the good or the beautiful, just as he ought to come to appreciate the very great difficulty of uniting them in life or art, which the lives and works of Pater and Hopkins illustrate. This was their ideal, however, and in espousing it, they affirmed that grand tradition of Humanism, which I believe to be the distinctive mark of Western culture, the quest to realize fully the Divine order of things and to rest in that holy state:

Beauty's bearing or muse of mounting vein,/ All, in this case, bathed in high hallowing grace. . . .[5]

Notes

References to the works I cite frequently will appear in the following abbreviated forms:

1. *The Letters of Gerard Manley Hopkins to Robert Bridges*, edited by C. C. Abbott (London: Oxford, 1935), as *Letters to Bridges*.
2. *The Correspondence of Gerard Manley Hopkins and Richard Watson Dixon*, edited by C. C. Abbott (London: Oxford, 1935), as *Letters to Dixon*.
3. *Further Letters of Gerard Manley Hopkins*, edited by C. C. Abbott (2d ed.; London: Oxford, 1956), as *Further Letters*.
4. *The Journals and Papers of Gerard Manley Hopkins*, edited by H. House and Graham Storey (London: Oxford, 1959), as *Journals*.
5. *Poems of Gerard Manley Hopkins*, edited by W. H. Gardner (3rd ed.; London: Oxford, 1948), as *Poems*.
6. Walter Pater, *Works* (London: Macmillan, 1910 Library Edition) by title of individual work.

CHAPTER ONE

1. Thomas Wright, *The Life of Walter Pater* (London, 1907), I, 98-99; William Sharp, *Papers and Personal Reminiscences* (London, 1912).
2. See "The Child in the House," in *Miscellaneous Studies*, pp. 181, 189-90, 195; *Poems*, p. 22.
3. Wright, I, 137.
4. "Diaphaneitè" in *Miscellaneous Studies*, p. 250.
5. *Ibid.*
6. *Ibid.*, p. 248.
7. *Letters to Bridges*, p. 225.

8. "Diaphaneitè," pp. 249-50.
9. *Ibid.*, p. 248.
10. *Ibid.*, p. 247
11. Wright, I, 137.
12. *Poems*, p. 43.
13. Wright, I, 109; see *Journals*, p. 72.

CHAPTER TWO

1. *Journals*, p. 133.
2. T. Humphry Ward, "Brasenose, 1864-1872," *Brasenose College Quartercentenary Monographs*, 1909, XIV, 2; pp. 74-75.
3. W. H. Pater, "Coleridge's Writings," *The Westminster Review* (January, 1866), XXIX, 107.
4. *Ibid.*
5. *Ibid.*, p. 108.
6. *Ibid.*, p. 129.
7. *Ibid.*, p. 127.
8. *Marius, The Epicurean*, II, 96. Hereafter cited as *Marius*.
9. *Journals*, p. 104.
10. *Ibid.*, p. 108; Edmund Gosse, *Critical Kit-Kats* (London, 1913), p. 262; *Journals*, pp. 110, 106.
11. *Journals*, pp.. 106-07.
12. *The Poets and Poetry of the Nineteenth Century*, ed. by Alfred H. Miles (London, 1906), p. 179.
13. *Journals*, p. 133.
14. *Further Letters*, pp. 215-217.
15. *Ibid.*, p. 224.
16. *Journals*, pp. 305-06.
17. *Ibid.*, p. 17.
18. *Ibid.*, p. 72.
19. *Ibid.*, p. 328.
20. Oxford Scrapbook in the Bodley Library (oxon. b. 147), p. 20. the Hexameron material is on p. 75. Pater is thought to have read his "*Diaphaneitè*" to this club. See A. C. Benson, *Pater*. English Men of Letters (New York, 1906), p. 10.
21. *Journals*, p. 138.
22. *Ibid.*, p. 353.
23. Gosse, p. 248.
24. *Further Letters*, p. 20.

25. *The Sermon and Devotional Writings of Gerard Manley Hopkins*, ed. Fr. Christopher Devlin, S.J. (London, 1959), Introduction, p. 5 ff. Hereafter *Devotional Writings.*

26. *Further Letters*, p. 38.

27. Benson, p. 26.

28. *Ibid.*, pp. 25-26.

29. *Further Letters*, p. 40.

30. See *Journals*, pp. 163-66.

31. *Ibid.*, p. 166.

32. Wright, II, 229-32.

33. Solomon did a portrait drawing of Pater in 1872; see *Journals*, p. 385.

34. *Journals*, p. 166.

35. *Letters to Bridges*, p. 24.

36. *Ibid.*, p. 39.

37. Graham Hough, *The Last Romantics*. University Paperbacks (London, 1961), p. xix.

38. Benson, p. 52.

39. Wright, II, 12.

40. W. H. Mallock, *The New Republic*, ed. by J. Max Patrick (Gainesville, 1950), p. 21.

41. *Ibid.*, p. 123.

42. *Ibid.*, p. 20.

43. *Ibid.*, p. 21.

44. *Ibid.*, pp. 123-29.

45. *Ibid.*, p. 169.

46. *Ibid.*

47. *Ibid.*, pp. 170-71.

48. *Ibid.*, p. 171.

49. *Ibid.*, p. 175

50. *Ibid.*, p. 176

51. *Ibid.*, p. 210

52. Benson, p. 53; Ferris Greenslet, *Walter Pater* (New York, 1903), p. 36; Wright, II, 18.

53. Benson, pp. 53-54.

54. Wright, II, 17-18.

55. Gosse, pp. 257-58.

56. Iain Fletcher, *Walter Pater* (London, 1959), p. 8.

57. See Benson, pp. 54-58.

58. *Further Letters*, p. 153.

59. *Letters to Bridges*, pp. 72-73.

60. *Ibid.*, p. 48.
61. *Ibid.*, p. 58
62. *Further Letters*, p. 151.
63. *Ibid.*, p. 246.
64. *Letters to Bridges*, pp. 224-25. D. A. Bischoff, S. J., thinks that the opportunities may well have increased once or twice according to his conjectures about Hopkins' visits to England from Dublin.
65. *The Renaissance*, p. 233.
66. See Lawrence G. Evans, "Some Letters of Walter Pater," unpublished dissertation (Harvard, 1961), pp. 19-20; 104; 92-93; 87-88.
67. *Further Letters*, p. 385.
68. G. Tillotson, "Pater, Mr. Rose, and the 'Conclusion' of the *Renaissance*," *Essays and Studies* (1946), XXXII, 50.

CHAPTER THREE

1. See unpublished dissertation (Harvard, 1961) by Lawrence G. Evans, "Some Letters of Walter Pater." I am heavily indebted in this chapter to Mr. Evans' collection and scholarship. References hereafter will be to *Letters* and citation, excepting commentary, will be by letter number.
2. *Letters*, 24.
3. *Letters*, 19, 20, 22, 23, 24, 25, 26, 27, 28.
4. *Letters*, 28.
5. *Letters*, 48.
6. *Letters*, 47.
7. *Letters*, 46, 47.
8. *Letters*, 48.
9. *Letters*, 50.
10. Gosse, p. 267.
11. *Letters*, 40.
12. See *Letters*, p. xxi, n. 1.
13. See *Letters*, p. xxiv, n. 1.
14. *Letters*, 59.
15. *Letters*, 61.
16. Letters, 63; Sharp, p. 212.
17. *Letters*, 65.
18. *Letters*, 67.
19. *Letters*, 72.

20. Arthur Symons, *Figures of Several Centuries* (London, 1916), pp. 332-33.

21. *Ibid.*, p. 331 including note.

22. *Letters*, p. 76, n. 1.

23. Wright, p. 101.

24. *Letters*, p. 76, n. 1.

25. *Gaston De Latour*, Preface, p. vii.

26. Benson, p. 140.

27. *Letters*, 76, 79, 80, 86.

28. *Letters*, 97, 98, 99, 100, 115.

29. *Letters*, 103, n. 2; 112, 119.

30. *Letters*, 105, 111, 113, 114, 116.

31. *Letters*, 120, 122.

32. *Letters*, 121.

33. *Letters*, 124.

34. *Letters to Dixon*, p. 90.

35. *Ibid.*, p. 93.

36. *Ibid.*, p. 94.

37. *Further Letters*, p. 231.

38. *Ibid.*, p. 408.

39. *Letters to Dixon*, p. 14.

40. See David A. Downes, *Gerard Manley Hopkins: A Study of His Ignatian Spirit* (New York, 1959), pp. 52-73.

41. *Journals*, pp. 125-30.

42. Hopkins told Dixon in 1881: "Suarez is our most famous theologian: he is a man of vast volume of mind, but without originality or brilliancy: he treats everything satisfactorily, but you never remember a phrase of his, the manner is nothing." *Letters to Dixon*, p. 95.

43. *Journals*, p. 221.

44. It is not pertinent here to discuss Hopkins and Scotus, but I refer the reader to the introductory essays in *Devotional Writings* and to illuminating essays in the *Month; N.S.*, III (1950), 114-27; 191-202.

45. *Letters to Bridges*, p. 319.

46. *Ibid.*, p. 160.

47. *Further Letters*, p. 243.

48. *Devotional Writings*, p. 54.

49. *Ibid.*, p. 58.

50. *Ibid.*, p. 62.

51. *Ibid.*, p. 68.
52. *Ibid.*, pp. 83-89.
53. *Ibid.*, p. 34.
54. *Ibid.*, p. 81.
55. *Ibid.*, p. 89.
56. *Letters to Dixon*, p. 33.
57. *Further Letters*, p. 157.
58. *Ibid.*, p. 244.
59. *Letters to Bridges*, p. 104.
60. *Ibid.*, p. 110. See also *Letters to Dixon*, p. 42, and *Further Letters*, p. 63.
61. *Ibid.*, p. 135.
62. *Letters to Dixon*, p. 75.
63. *Letters to Bridges*, p. 138.
64. His notes suggest an application of Scotus and more than a little Suarez to Ignatian spirituality. As was usual with Hopkins, his highly individualizing touch is apparent. For his theology, see Fr. Christopher Devlin's essay in *Devotional Writings*, pp. 107-21. For Ignatian spirituality, see Downes, pp. 26-51.
65. *Letters to Bridges*, p. 175.
66. *Devotional Writings*, p. 146.
67. *Letters to Bridges*, p. 150.
68. *Ibid.*
69. *Further Letters*, p. 251.
70. *Devotional Writings*, pp. 253-54.
71. *Poems*, p. 109.
72. *Letters to Bridges*, p. 190.
73. *Further Letters*, p. 256.
74. *Poems.* pp. 103-11.
75. *Letters to Bridges*, p. 270.
76. *Devotional Writings*, pp. 261-71.
77. *Ibid.*, p. 221.
78. *Further Letters*, p. 197.
79. *Letters to Dixon*, p. 14.
80. *Ibid.*, p. 138.

Chapter Four

1. *Further Letters*, pp. 202, 204.
2. *Letters to Bridges*, pp. 30-31.

3. Christopher Dawson, *Religion and Culture* (New York, 1948), p. 29.

4. Gerald A. McCool, "The Primacy of Intuition," *Thought* (Spring, 1962), pp. 63, 64.

5. William James, *Varieties of Religious Experience* (New York, 1902), p. 58.

6. Josef Pieper, *Scholasticism* (New York, 1960), p. 24.

7. *Ibid.*, p. 25.

8. *Ibid.*, p. 44.

9. Etienne Gilson, *History of the Middle Ages* (New York, 1955), pp. 410-11.

10. *Letters to Dixon*, p. 95.

11. W. H. Gardner, "Anvil-Ding and Tongue That Told," *Month* (February, 1961), pp. 92-93.

12. *Ibid.*, p. 92.

13. *Ibid.*, p. 93.

14. Pieper, pp. 51-54.

15. *Ibid.*, pp. 125-26.

16. *Letters to Bridges*, p. 225.

17. Pieper, pp. 143-44.

18. See Fr. Christopher Devlin, "The Image and the Word," *Month* (February and March, 1950).

19. See Fr. Christopher Devlin, "An Essay on Scotus," *Month* (November-December, 1946).

20. *Devotional Writings*, p. 136.

21. *Ibid.*, pp. 349-51.

22. *Poems*, p. 84.

23. *Journals*, p. 221.

24. *Ibid.*, p. 71.

25. *Devotional Writings*, pp. 200-01; 253-54; 120.

26. Gardner, p. 90.

27. W. H. Pater, "Coleridge's Writings," *The Westminster Review* (January, 1866), p. 107.

28. *Plato and Platonism*, pp. 139-40.

29. *The Renaissance*, p. 49.

30. "Coleridge's Writings," p. 111.

31. *Plato and Platonism*, p. 124.

32. *Ibid.*, p. 174.

33. *Ibid.*, p. 187.

34. Lord David Cecil, *The Art of Reading* (New York, 1957), p. 265.

35. *The Renaissance*, Preface, pp. xiii-xv.

36. *Ibid.*, p. 2.

37. *Ibid.*, p. 31.

38. *Ibid.*, p. 33.

39. *Ibid.*, p. 204.

40. *Ibid.*

41. See Dawson, p. 49.

42. *The Renaissance*, p. 219.

43. *Ibid.*, p. 224.

44. *Ibid.*, p. 226.

45. *Ibid.*, p. 205.

46. *Ibid.*, p. 227.

47. *Plato and Platonism*, p. 23.

48. *Letters to Bridges*, p. 27; 273.

49. *Letters to Dixon*, p. 97.

50. *Further Letters*, p. 366.

51. R. V. Osbourn, "Marius The Epicurean," *Essays in Criticism* (October, 1951), pp. 400-02.

52. Henri Daniel-Rops, *The Church of Apostles and Martyrs* (New York, 1962), I, 255-58.

53. *Marius*, I, 135-36.

54. See the following as current instances of this philosophic insight: Karl Rahner, *Geist in Welt* (Munich, 1957); C. Cirne-Lima, *Der Personale Glaube* (Innsbruck, 1959).

55. *Marius*, II, 39.

56. *Ibid.*, I, 232.

57. *Ibid.*, pp. 63-64.

58. *Poems*, p. 57.

59. *Marius*, II, 64.

60. *Ibid.*, p. 65.

61. See John Henry Cardinal Newman, *A Grammar of Assent* (New York, 1955), Chapter 9.

62. *Marius*, II, 67.

63. *Poems*, p. 33.

64. *Marius*, II, 68.

65. *Ibid.*, p. 70.

66. *Ibid.*, p. 71.

67. *Ibid.*

68. *Ibid.*

69. *Ibid.*, p. 72.

70. See Osbourn, "Marius The Epicurean," pp. 398-400.

Index